AMERICANS WITH DISABILITIES ACT

by

Margaret C. Jasper

Oceana's Legal Almanac Series:
Law for the Layperson

Oceana®

NEW YORK

5-13-2008
WW
$ 39.95

OXFORD
UNIVERSITY PRESS

*Oxford University Press, Inc., publishes works that further Oxford University's
objective of excellence in research, scholarship, and education.*

Copyright © 2008 by Oxford University Press, Inc.
Published by Oxford University Press, Inc.
198 Madison Avenue, New York, New York 10016

Library of Congress Cataloging-in-Publication Data

Jasper, Margaret C.
    Americans with Disabilities Act / by Margaret C. Jasper. -- 2nd ed.
    p. cm. -- (Oceana's legal almanac series: law for the layperson)
    Summary: "Focuses on the Americans with Disabilities Act (ADA) and the rights
of the disabled under this Act. Also explored are the areas covered by the ADA,
specifically employment, transportation, public accommodations, State and local
government services, and telecommunications. For areas not covered by the ADA,
a review of other pertinent legislation is provided"--Provided by publisher.
    Includes bibliographical references.
    ISBN 978-0-19-533897-3 ((clothbound) : alk. paper)   1. People with disabili-
ties--Legal status, laws, etc.--United States--Popular works.   2. Discrimination
against people with disabilities--Law and legislation--United States--Popular
works.   3. United States. Americans with Disabilities Act of 1990--Popular works.
I. Title.
    KF480.Z9J37 2008
    342.7308'7--dc22   2007043764

Note to Readers:

You may order this or any other Oxford University Press publication
by visiting the Oxford University Press website at www.oup.com

To My Husband Chris

Your love and support

are my motivation and inspiration

To My Sons, Michael, Nick and Chris

-and-

In memory of my son, Jimmy

Table of Contents

CHAPTER 3:
TITLE II - PUBLIC SERVICES

CHAPTER 4:
TITLE III - PUBLIC ACCOMMODATIONS AND SERVICES
OPERATED BY PRIVATE ENTITIES

ABOUT THE AUTHOR

MARGARET C. JASPER is an attorney engaged in the general practice of law in South Salem, New York, concentrating in the areas of personal injury and entertainment law. Ms. Jasper holds a Juris Doctor degree from Pace University School of Law, White Plains, New York, is a member of the New York and Connecticut bars, and is certified to practice before the United States District Courts for the Southern and Eastern Districts of New York, the United States Court of Appeals for the Second Circuit, and the United States Supreme Court.

Ms. Jasper has been appointed to the law guardian panel for the Family Court of the State of New York, is a member of a number of professional organizations and associations, and is a New York State licensed real estate broker operating as Jasper Real Estate, in South Salem, New York.

Margaret Jasper maintains a website at http://www.JasperLawOffice.com.

In 2004, Ms. Jasper successfully argued a case before the New York Court of Appeals, which gives mothers of babies who are stillborn due to medical negligence, the right to bring a legal action and recover emotional distress damages. This successful appeal overturned a 26-year old New York case precedent, which previously prevented mothers of stillborn babies from suing their negligent medical providers.

Ms. Jasper is the author and general editor of the following legal Almanacs:

AIDS Law

The Americans with Disabilities Act

Animal Rights Law

Auto Leasing

Bankruptcy Law for the Individual Debtor

Banks and their Customers

Becoming a Citizen

Buying and Selling Your Home

Commercial Law

Consumer Rights and the Law

Co-ops and Condominiums: Your Rights and Obligations As Owner

Copyright Law

Credit Cards and the Law

Custodial Rights

Dealing with Debt

Dictionary of Selected Legal Terms

Drunk Driving Law

DWI, DUI and the Law

Education Law

Elder Law

Employee Rights in the Workplace

Employment Discrimination Under Title VII

Environmental Law

Estate Planning

Everyday Legal Forms

Executors and Personal Representatives: Rights and Responsibilities

Guardianship and the Law

Harassment in the Workplace

Health Care and Your Rights

Health Care Directives

Hiring Household Help and Contractors: Your Rights and Obligations Under the Law

Home Mortgage Law Primer

Hospital Liability Law

How To Change Your Name

How To Form an LLC

How To Protect Your Challenged Child

How To Start Your Own Business

Identity Theft and How To Protect Yourself

Individual Bankruptcy and Restructuring

Injured on the Job: Employee Rights, Worker's Compensation and Disability Insurance Law

International Adoption

Juvenile Justice and Children's Law

Labor Law

Landlord-Tenant Law

Law for the Small Business Owner

The Law of Adoption

The Law of Attachment and Garnishment

The Law of Buying and Selling

The Law of Capital Punishment

The Law of Child Custody

The Law of Contracts

The Law of Debt Collection

The Law of Dispute Resolution

The Law of Immigration

The Law of Libel and Slander

The Law of Medical Malpractice

The Law of No-Fault Insurance

The Law of Obscenity and Pornography

The Law of Personal Injury

The Law of Premises Liability

The Law of Product Liability

The Law of Speech and the First Amendment

Lemon Laws

Living Together: Practical Legal Issues

Marriage and Divorce

Missing and Exploited Children: How to Protect Your Child

Motor Vehicle Law

Nursing Home Negligence

Patent Law

Pet Law

Prescription Drugs

Privacy and the Internet: Your Rights and Expectations Under the Law

Probate Law

Protecting Your Business: Disaster Preparation and the Law

Real Estate Law for the Homeowner and Broker

Religion and the Law

Retirement Planning

The Right to Die

Rights of Single Parents

Small Claims Court

Social Security Law

Special Education Law

Teenagers and Substance Abuse

Trademark Law

Trouble Next Door: What to do With Your Neighbor

Victim's Rights Law

Violence Against Women

Welfare: Your Rights and the Law

What if It Happened to You: Violent Crimes and Victims' Rights

What if the Product Doesn't Work: Warranties & Guarantees

Workers' Compensation Law

Your Child's Legal Rights: An Overview

Your Rights in a Class Action Suit

Your Rights as a Tenant

Your Rights Under the Family and Medical Leave Act

You've Been Fired: Your Rights and Remedies

INTRODUCTION

In the past, disabled individuals have faced a wide variety of obstacles that prevented them from fully participating in all that American society has to offer. They have struggled with obtaining employment, and have been denied access to many services most Americans take for granted. Due to bias, insensitivity and plain ignorance, the disabled have been subjected to discrimination and intolerance.

Acknowledging that disabled persons are as equally entitled to participate in society as non-disabled Americans, the federal government intervened to provide the disabled with effective legislation to enforce their rights. In 1990, Congress passed the Americans with Disabilities Act (ADA) in order to give civil rights protections to individuals with disabilities similar to those prohibiting discrimination on the basis of race, color, sex, national origin, age, and religion.

The ADA's purpose is to guarantee equal opportunity for the disabled with respect to employment, transportation, public accommodations, state and local government services, and telecommunications. By removing the impediments, society will benefit from the talents and skills disabled persons have to offer. In addition, by making services and accommodations—such as retail stores, hotels and restaurants—more accessible, the disabled will become an increasingly significant factor in the marketplace, and an asset to the economy.

This Almanac examines the ADA, and discusses the rights disabled individuals are entitled to under the Act. The areas governed by the ADA are explored, including employment, transportation, public accommodations, state and local government services, and telecommunications. This Almanac also gives a brief overview of legislation designed to protect the disabled in areas not covered by the ADA.

The Appendix provides selected provisions of the ADA, sample forms, and other pertinent information and data. The Glossary contains definitions of many of the terms used throughout the Almanac.

CHAPTER 1:
AN OVERVIEW OF THE AMERICANS WITH DISABILITIES ACT

IN GENERAL

Recognizing that disabled persons are entitled to civil rights protections such as those already provided to individuals who are discriminated against on the basis of race, color, sex, national origin, age, and religion, the federal government has endeavored to provide disabled persons with effective legislation to enforce their civil rights. The most significant piece of legislation passed by Congress to protect and promote the rights of the disabled was the Americans with Disabilities Act of 1990 (the "ADA").

Tables indicating the percent of people with a disability, by age and state, are set forth in Appendices 1 through 3.

STRUCTURE OF THE ADA

The ADA is divided into five sections, known as "Titles." It provides for equal opportunity for all persons in the areas of employment (Title I); public services (Title II); public accommodations (Title III); and telecommunications (Title IV). The ADA was originally enacted in public law format and later rearranged and published by subject matter in the United States Code. The United States Code is divided into "titles" numbered 1 through 50. Titles I, II, III and V of the ADA have been codified in Title 42 of the United States Code, beginning at section 12101. Title IV of the original public law format has been codified in Title 47 – Telegraphs, Telephones, and Radiotelegraphs of the United States Code.

Selected provisions of the Americans with Disabilities Act as codified in the U.S. Code at 42 U.S.C. §12101 et seq (original public law sections in brackets) are set forth in Appendix 4.

Subchapter I [Title I]: Employment

Subchapter I [Title I] requires employers with 15 or more employees to provide qualified individuals with disabilities an equal opportunity to benefit from the full range of employment-related opportunities available to others. For example, it prohibits discrimination in recruitment, hiring, promotions, training, pay, social activities, and other privileges of employment. It restricts questions that can be asked about an applicant's disability before a job offer is made, and it requires that employers make reasonable accommodation to the known physical or mental limitations of otherwise qualified individuals with disabilities, unless it results in undue hardship. Religious entities with 15 or more employees are covered under Title I.

Title I is discussed in more detail in Chapter 2, Title I – Employment, of this Almanac.

Subchapter II [Title II]: Public Services

Public Entities

Subchapter II [Title II] covers all activities of state and local governments regardless of the government entity's size or receipt of Federal funding. Title II requires that state and local governments give people with disabilities an equal opportunity to benefit from all of their programs, services, and activities, including public education, employment, transportation, recreation, health care, social services, courts, voting, and town meetings.

State and local governments are required to follow specific architectural standards in the new construction and alteration of their buildings. They also must relocate programs or otherwise provide access in inaccessible older buildings, and communicate effectively with people who have hearing, vision, or speech disabilities. Public entities are not required to take actions that would result in undue financial and administrative burdens. They are required to make reasonable modifications to policies, practices, and procedures where necessary to avoid discrimination, unless they can demonstrate that doing so would fundamentally alter the nature of the service, program, or activity being provided.

Public Transportation

The transportation provisions of Title II cover public transportation services, such as city buses and public rail transit, including subways, commuter rails, and Amtrak. Public transportation authorities may not discriminate against people with disabilities in the provision of their services. They must comply with requirements for accessibility in newly purchased vehicles, make good faith efforts to purchase or lease accessible used buses, remanufacture buses in an accessible manner, and, unless it would result in an undue burden, provide paratransit where they operate fixed-route bus or rail systems. Paratransit is a service where individuals who are unable to use the regular transit system independently, because of a physical or mental impairment, are picked up and dropped off at their destinations.

This section is discussed in more detail in Chapter 3, Title II – Public Services, of this Almanac

Subchapter III [Title III]: Public Accommodations and Services Operated by Private Entities

Subchapter III [Title III] covers businesses and nonprofit service providers that are public accommodations, privately operated entities offering certain types of courses and examinations, privately operated transportation, and commercial facilities. Public accommodations are private entities who own, lease, lease to, or operate facilities such as restaurants, retail stores, hotels, movie theaters, private schools, convention centers, doctors' offices, homeless shelters, transportation depots, zoos, funeral homes, day care centers, and recreation facilities including sports stadiums and fitness clubs. Transportation services provided by private entities are also covered by this section.

Public accommodations must comply with basic nondiscrimination requirements that prohibit exclusion, segregation, and unequal treatment. They also must comply with specific requirements related to architectural standards for new and altered buildings; reasonable modifications to policies, practices, and procedures; effective communication with people with hearing, vision, or speech disabilities; and other access requirements. Additionally, public accommodations must remove barriers in existing buildings where it is easy to do so without much difficulty or expense, given the public accommodation's resources.

Courses and examinations related to professional, educational, or trade-related applications, licensing, certifications, or credentialing must be provided in a place and manner accessible to people with disabilities, or alternative accessible arrangements must be offered.

Commercial facilities, such as factories and warehouses, must comply with the ADA's architectural standards for new construction and alterations.

Title III is discussed in more detail in Chapter 4, Title III – Public Accommodations and Services Operated By Private Entities of this Almanac.

Title 47 - Secs. 225 and 611 [Title IV]: Telegraphs, Telephones, and Radiotelegraphs

Sections 225 and 611 of Title 47 [Title IV] addresses telephone and television access for people with hearing and speech disabilities. It requires common carriers (telephone companies) to establish interstate and intrastate telecommunications relay services (TRS) 24 hours a day, 7 days a week. TRS enables callers with hearing and speech disabilities who use telecommunications devices for the deaf (TDDs), which are also known as teletypewriters (TTYs), and callers who use voice telephones to communicate with each other through a third party communications assistant. The Federal Communications Commission (FCC) has set minimum standards for TRS services. Title IV also requires closed captioning of Federally funded public service announcements.

This section is discussed in more detail in Chapter 5, Title IV – Telecommunications, of this Almanac.

Subchapter IV [Title V]: Miscellaneous Provisions

Subchapter IV [Title V] of the ADA contains provisions regarding the construction of the statute (Section 501); state immunity (Section 502); a prohibition against retaliation and coercion (Section 503); regulations by the Architectural and Transportation Barriers Compliance Board (Section 504); a provision for attorney's fees (Section 505); provisions for technical assistance and implementation of the Act (Section 506); provisions governing federal wilderness areas (Section 507); application of the ADA to transvestites (Section 508); coverage of Congress and the Legislative Branch (Section 509); provisions relating to the illegal use of drugs (Section 510); miscellaneous definitions (Section 511); amendments to the Rehabilitation Act (Section 512); availability of alternative means of dispute resolution (Section 513); and severability provisions (Section 514).

This section is discussed in more detail in Chapter 6, Title V – Miscellaneous Provisions, of this Almanac.

DISABLED PERSONS

The ADA is targeted primarily at protecting disabled individuals. Under the Act, an individual is considered "disabled" if:

1. The person is substantially impaired with respect to a major life activity;

2. The person has a record of such an impairment; or

3. The person is regarded as having such an impairment.

Covered physical or mental disabilities may include visual, speech or hearing impairments, orthopedic conditions, epilepsy, cerebral palsy, muscular dystrophy, multiple sclerosis, cancer, heart disease, diabetes, mental retardation, emotional illness, certain learning disabilities, AIDS/HIV disease, tuberculosis, past drug addiction, and alcoholism.

In addition to disabled individuals, the Act also protects:

1. Persons who have an association with an individual known to have a disability, such as a relative; and

2. Persons who have been coerced or subjected to retaliation because they helped a disabled person assert his or her rights under the ADA.

A directory of national disability organizations is set forth in Appendix 5.

JURISDICTION

Federal Government

The ADA covers Congress and other entities in the legislative branch of the Federal Government. The ADA does not cover the executive branch of the Federal Government, which continues to be covered by Title V of the Rehabilitation Act of 1973. The Rehabilitation Act prohibits discrimination against the handicapped in employment and services, and served as a model for the ADA. The Rehabilitation Act is further discussed in Chapter 7, Law Enforcement Under The ADA, of this Almanac.

State and Local Governments

The ADA covers state and local governments, and their departments, agencies, or other instrumentalities. Unlike section 504 of the Rehabilitation Act, which only covers programs receiving Federal financial assistance, the ADA extends to all the activities of state and local governments whether or not they receive Federal funds.

The Equal Employment Opportunity Commission

The Equal Employment Opportunity Commission ("EEOC") is a federal agency responsible for issuing regulations to enforce the provisions of Title I of the ADA, under the same procedures now applicable to race, color, sex, national origin, and religious discrimination under Title VII of the Civil Rights Act of 1964, as amended, and the Civil Rights Act of 1991.

The Department of Justice

The Department of Justice ("DOJ") is a federal agency responsible for issuing regulations under Titles II and III of the ADA, and for providing technical assistance and enforcement.

A directory of federal agencies governing ADA compliance is set forth in Appendix 6.

CHAPTER 2:
TITLE I - EMPLOYMENT

IN GENERAL

Title I of the Americans with Disabilities Act (ADA) addresses the rights of individuals with disabilities in employment settings. According to the U.S. Department of Justice, the purpose of Title I is to ensure that qualified individuals with disabilities are protected from discrimination on the basis of disability. As long as the individual is qualified for an employment opportunity, that person cannot be denied that opportunity simply because he or she has a disability, and must therefore be given the same consideration for employment that individuals without disabilities are given

COVERED EMPLOYERS

The Title I employment provisions apply to private employers, state and local governments, employment agencies, educational institutions, and labor unions. Employers with 25 or more employees were covered as of July 26, 1992. Employers with 15 or more employees were covered two years later, beginning July 26, 1994.

PROHIBITED PRACTICES

The ADA prohibits discrimination in all employment practices, including job application procedures, hiring, firing, advancement, compensation, training, and other terms, conditions, and privileges of employment. It applies to recruitment, advertising, tenure, layoff, leave, fringe benefits, and all other employment-related activities.

COVERED PERSONS

Employment discrimination is prohibited against "qualified individuals with disabilities." This includes applicants for employment and employees.

Disability Defined

An individual with disabilities is defined as:

1. A person who has a physical or mental impairment that substantially limits one or more major life activities;

2. A person who has a record of such an impairment; or

3. A person who is regarded as having such an impairment.

Under the first part of the definition, the person must have an impairment that must substantially limit his or her major life activities such as seeing, hearing, speaking, walking, breathing, performing manual tasks, learning, caring for oneself, and working.

Thus, an individual with epilepsy, paralysis, HIV infection, AIDS, a substantial hearing or visual impairment, mental retardation, or a specific learning disability is covered, but an individual with a minor, non-chronic condition of short duration, such as a sprain, broken limb, or the flu, generally would not be covered.

For example, an employee suffers a broken wrist that is expected to heal, but while it is healing he is unable to perform the essential functions of his job as an assembly-line worker. This employee is not protected by the ADA because, although he is "impaired," the impairment does not substantially limit a major life activity because it is of limited duration and will have no long-term effect.

Under the second part of the definition, an individual with a "record" of a disability would cover a person who has recovered from an impairment that substantially limited his or her major life activities, such as cancer or mental illness.

Under the third part of the definition, individuals who are regarded as having a substantially limiting impairment, even though they may not have such an impairment, are protected. For example, this provision would protect a qualified individual with a severe facial disfigurement from being denied employment because an employer feared the "negative reactions" of customers or co-workers.

In addition, employees who are discriminated against because they know, are associated with, or are related to a disabled individual are also protected from adverse action caused by bias or ignorance concerning certain disabilities. For example, if an employee's family member suffers from a disease, such as AIDS, he or she should not suffer job discrimination due to the ignorant assumption that AIDS can be transmitted through casual contact.

Qualified Individual

To be covered by the ADA, the disabled person must be "qualified"— i.e., he or she must meet the legitimate experience, education, or other requirements of the position he or she holds or is applying for, and must be able to perform the "essential functions" of the position, with or without "reasonable accommodations." This includes applicants for employment as well as employees.

Essential Functions

The law requires that the disabled individual must be able to perform the "essential functions" of the job. The term "essential" was used so that individuals would not be deemed unqualified merely because they are unable to perform incidental or inconsequential tasks related to the position.

Essential functions are the basic tasks that an employee must be able to perform, with or without reasonable accommodation. Prior to advertising for an open position, an employer should carefully examine each job description to determine which functions or tasks are essential to performance.

The essential functions of a particular job may depend on an evaluation of the following factors:

1. Whether the existence of the position is for the purposes of performing the function;

2. The degree of expertise or skill required to perform the particular function; and

3. The number of other employees available to perform the function or assist in performing the function.

If a complaint is brought and the EEOC investigates, a written job description which carefully describes the essential functions of the position, and which was prepared prior to advertising for the position, will weigh in the employer's favor.

REASONABLE ACCOMMODATIONS

If an individual is qualified to perform the essential job functions, except for certain limitations caused by their disability, the employer is obliged to consider whether the individual could perform these functions if "reasonable accommodations" are provided.

The guidelines promulgated by the EEOC provide that an employer must make a reasonable effort to provide an appropriate reasonable accommodation for a qualified disabled employee who requests one. A reasonable accommodation is any modification or adjustment to the work environment that will enable a qualified disabled individual to perform the essential job functions.

A reasonable accommodation must also be made to enable a disabled individual to participate in the job application process, and to enjoy the benefits and privileges of employment equal to those available to other employees.

Reasonable accommodations may include:

1. Acquiring or modifying equipment or devices;

2. Job restructuring;

3. Providing part-time or modified work schedules;

4. Adjusting or modifying examinations, training materials or policies; and

5. Providing readers and interpreters.

If the employee is unable to perform the "essential functions" of his or her position—and there are no reasonable accommodations that would enable the employee to function in that position—a reasonable accommodation may include reassignment to another available position.

However, an employer is not required to find a disabled employee alternative employment if it is not reasonably available. In that case, the disabled employee would not be "qualified" because he or she does not meet the requirements of the position, and is unable to perform the essential functions of the position, with or without a reasonable accommodation. In addition, if an employee refuses to accept an offered accommodation, the individual may likewise be considered not "qualified."

As discussed below, a reasonable accommodation may also include making the workplace readily accessible to and usable by disabled persons. For example, it would be a "reasonable accommodation" for an employer to permit a wheelchair bound employee to adjust his or her work hours so that they he or she is not traveling during rush hour.

Disclosure

Because an employer is only required to accommodate a "known" disability of a qualified applicant or employee, the employee must disclose that he or she has a disability which is covered under the statute, and requires a "reasonable accommodation."

Undue Hardship

Despite the requirement to provide reasonable accommodations, an employer is not required to provide a reasonable accommodation that would pose an "undue hardship" on the business.

An undue hardship is defined as an "action requiring significant difficulty or expense" when considered in light of a number of factors, such as the cost of the accommodation in relation to the resources of the employer, or whether the accommodation would fundamentally alter the nature or operation of the business. A large employer with greater resources would be expected to make more extensive accommodations than would be required of a smaller employer.

If a particular accommodation would be an undue hardship, the employer must try to identify another accommodation that would not pose such a hardship. If the cost of the accommodation is prohibitive, the following alternatives may be considered:

1. Whether there is funding available from an outside source, such as a vocational rehabilitation agency;

2. Whether the cost of providing the accommodation can be offset by state or federal tax credits or deductions; or

3. Whether the applicant or employee will provide the accommodation, or is willing to contribute towards the cost.

Direct Threat

An employer does not have to hire an individual who poses a "direct threat" to his or her health or safety, or the health and safety of others, if the risk cannot be eliminated or significantly reduced by means of a reasonable accommodation.

A direct threat is defined as one that carries with it a significant risk of substantial harm, not a slightly increased risk or a speculative or remote risk. If the employer claims that a direct threat exists, he or she must substantiate that the risk is real and not merely a perceived threat. Such proof may include objective medical evidence that there is a significant risk that substantial harm could occur in the workplace.

For example, transmission of AIDS/HIV disease will rarely be a legitimate "direct threat" because it has been medically established that the illness cannot be transmitted by casual contact. AIDS/HIV disease can only be transmitted by sexual contact with an infected individual, exposure to infected blood or blood products, or perinatally from an infected mother to her infant during pregnancy, birth or breastfeeding. Thus, there is little possibility the illness could ever be transmitted in a workplace setting.

ACCESSIBILITY

The employer's obligation under Title I is to provide access for an individual applicant to participate in the job application process, and for an individual employee with a disability to perform the essential functions of his/her job, including access to a building, to the work site, to needed equipment, and to all facilities used by employees.

For example, if an employee lounge is located in a place inaccessible to an employee using a wheelchair, the lounge might be modified or relocated, or comparable facilities might be provided in a location that would enable the individual to take a break with co-workers. The employer must provide such access unless it would cause an undue hardship.

Under Title I, an employer is not required to make its existing facilities accessible until a particular applicant or employee with a particular disability needs an accommodation, and then the modifications should meet that individual's work needs. However, employers should consider initiating changes that will provide general accessibility, particularly for job applicants, since it is likely that people with disabilities will be applying for jobs.

The United States of America v. the Board of Education of the City of Chicago

This issue arose in a complaint with the U.S. Department of Justice against the Board of Education of the City of Chicago under Title I of the Americans with Disabilities Act. According to the charge filed with the Equal Employment Opportunity Commission (EEOC), a teacher alleged that the Board of Education violated Title I of the ADA by refusing to accommodate his disability—arthritis.

The teacher was assigned to a class located on the third floor of the school building. His duties required him to escort his class up and down three flights of stairs to various activities held in the basement. He requested relocation of his class from the third floor to the first or second floor as an accommodation for his disability. His request was denied and, as a result, he was forced to resign from his position and retire.

The parties subsequently entered into a settlement agreement. The Chicago Board of Education agreed to provide the teacher with a monetary settlement of $20,599.22 as compensatory damages for injuries sustained as a result of the Board's actions. The teacher did not seek job relief or reinstatement.

The text of the settlement agreement between the United States of America and the Chicago Board of Education is set forth in Appendix 7, Settlement Agreement Between The United States of America and The Board of Education of The City of Chicago – Public Accommodations.

Accessibility Under Title I and Title III Differentiated

Nevertheless, the accessibility requirement under Title I is different from that required under Title III concerning public accommodations. In the context of employment, accessibility must be provided to enable a qualified applicant to participate in the application process, to enable a qualified individual to perform essential job functions and to enable an employee with a disability to enjoy benefits and privileges available to other employees. The employer does not have to make changes to provide access in places or facilities that will not be used by that individual for employment-related activities or benefits.

However, if the business is also a place of public accommodation, the accessibility requirements for the general public under Title III would also apply. The accessibility guidelines under Title III are further discussed in Chapter 4, Title III – Public Accommodations and Services Operated By Private Entities, of this Almanac.

PREFERENTIAL TREATMENT

The law does not require the employer to give the disabled applicant or employee any preferential treatment over other applicants or employees. Employers are free to select the most qualified individual available provided those decisions are based on reasons unrelated to the disability.

For example, suppose two persons apply for a job as a typist and an essential function of the job is to type 75 words per minute accurately. One applicant, an individual with a disability, who is provided with a reasonable accommodation for a typing test, types 50 words per minute; the other applicant who has no disability accurately types 75 words per minute. The employer can hire the applicant with the higher typing speed, if typing speed is needed for successful performance of the job.

TAX CREDITS AND DEDUCTIONS

A special tax credit is available to help smaller employers make accommodations required by the ADA. An eligible small business may take a tax credit of up to $5,000 per year for accommodations made to comply with the ADA. The credit is available for one-half the cost of "eligible access expenditures" that are more than $250 but less than $10,250.

A full tax deduction, up to $15,000 per year, is also available to any business for expenses of removing qualified architectural or transportation barriers. Expenses covered include costs of removing barriers created by steps, narrow doors, inaccessible parking spaces, restroom facilities, and transportation vehicles.

RECORDKEEPING REQUIREMENT

The ADA requires an employer to maintain records, including: (i) job application forms; (ii) all records related to hiring; (iii) requests for reasonable accommodations, (iv) promotion, demotion, transfer, lay-off or termination records; (v) compensation schedules; and (vi) training or apprenticeship selection records.

Records are to be maintained for a period of one year after either: (i) the record is made; or (ii) the particular action is taken, whichever occurs later. However, if a charge of discrimination is filed or an action is brought by the EEOC, an employer must save all personnel records related to the charge until its final disposition.

NOTICE REQUIREMENT

The ADA requires employers to post a notice describing the ADA and its provisions, in an accessible format, available to all applicants, employees and members of labor organizations. The EEOC provides posters summarizing these and other Federal legal requirements for nondiscrimination. The EEOC also provides guidance to employers on making this information available in accessible formats for people who have disabilities preventing them from reading the notice, such as sight-impaired individuals.

MEDICAL EXAMINATIONS

Under Title I, an employer cannot require a job applicant to submit to a medical examination prior to making a job offer. An employer is also prohibited from asking the applicant about the existence, nature or severity of a disability, although an applicant may be questioned about his or her ability to perform specific job functions.

Nevertheless, a job offer may be conditioned on the results of a medical examination if the examination is required for all prospective employees in similar jobs.

Employment may thus be conditioned upon a satisfactory medical examination once the job offer is made. Nevertheless, if the results of the medical examination reveal a disability, the employer must still hire the individual unless the disability is employment-related, and no reasonable accommodations are available that would enable the applicant to perform the essential functions of the position.

Once an applicant is hired, an employer cannot require a medical examination, or ask the employee about his or her disability, unless it can be shown that these requirements are job related and necessary for the conduct of the business. Nevertheless, an employer may conduct voluntary medical examinations under an employee health program.

The results of any medical examinations, or other information gathered concerning an employee's disability, must be kept confidential, and maintained in a separate medical file.

Drug and Alcohol Addiction

The prohibition against pre-job offer medical examinations does not apply to testing for illegal drug use. An employee or applicant who "currently" uses illegal drugs is excluded from the definition of a "qualified" individual with a disability, and thus not protected by the ADA.

However, the ADA does not exclude (i) individuals who have successfully completed a drug rehabilitation program—or who are currently in such a program—and are no longer illegally using drugs; and (ii) individuals erroneously regarded as engaging in the illegal use of drugs.

An individual suffering from alcoholism is considered a person with a disability protected by the ADA, even if currently consuming alcohol, provided he or she is qualified to perform the essential functions of the job. Nevertheless, the employer is free to fire or otherwise discipline an alcoholic employee if their addiction adversely affects their job performance or conduct. The employer can further require that the alcoholic employee refrain from drinking alcohol while on the job.

FILING A COMPLAINT UNDER TITLE I OF THE ADA

The Equal Employment Opportunity Commission (EEOC) is responsible for issuing regulations to enforce the provisions of Title I of the ADA. Complaints may be filed with the EEOC or the designated state human rights agency. The EEOC operates 51 field offices throughout the country.

The appropriate office may be located by calling the EEOC. You may contact EEOC Headquarters as follows:

U.S. Equal Employment Opportunity Commission
1801 L Street, N.W.
Washington, D.C. 20507
Phone: (202) 663-4900
TTY: (202) 663-4494
Internet: http://www.eeoc.gov/
You can be automatically connected to your nearest Field
Office by calling:
Phone: 1-800-669-4000
TTY: 1-800-669-6820

A charge of discrimination must be filed within 180 days of the discriminatory act, unless there is a state or local law that also provides relief for discrimination on the basis of disability. In those cases, the complainant has 300 days to file a charge.

The Commission will investigate and attempt to resolve the charge through conciliation, following the same procedures used to handle charges of discrimination filed under Title VII of the Civil Rights Act of 1964.

In order to bring a discrimination claim, one must: (i) be a "qualified individual" with a recognized disability; and (ii) have suffered an adverse employment decision. However, meeting these two criteria does not guarantee that the individual will prevail on his or her claim.

An employer has the right to discharge or otherwise sanction a disabled employee for any reason other than for discriminatory reasons. Disability discrimination is very dependent upon the facts of each individual situation. Thus, it is crucial that the individual document the facts surrounding the alleged discriminatory act. The ADA prohibits an employer from retaliating against an applicant or employee for asserting his rights under the ADA.

One is also advised to seek consultation with a lawyer experienced in this area so that any legitimate claims may be presented in a timely fashion. Certain statutes have time requirements that must be met or the claim will be barred. The reader is advised to check the law of his or her own jurisdiction concerning time limitations. A claim that is not filed within the required time period will likely be barred.

Under the ADA, if the individual decides to proceed with a civil lawsuit against the employer, the action must be filed within ninety days after receipt of the EEOC "right to sue" letter.

An individual who prevails in his or her discrimination claim under the ADA is generally entitled to recover:

1. The economic losses that would have been earned if the discrimination had not taken place, including back pay, front pay, a promotion or benefits;

2. Reasonable accommodations;

3. Damages for emotional trauma and any associated physical suffering; and

4. Attorney fees and costs.

In addition, compensatory and punitive damages may also be available in cases of intentional discrimination or where an employer fails to make a good faith effort to provide a reasonable accommodation.

Because state law may provide even greater compensation to the victim, the reader is again advised to check the law of his or her jurisdiction in this regard.

THE EEOC TECHNICAL ASSISTANCE PROGRAM

In order to assist employers in complying with the provisions of Title II of the ADA, the EEOC conducts a technical assistance program designed to help employers understand their responsibilities. The program also assists disabled individuals in understanding their rights under the law.

The EEOC's technical assistance program is separate and distinct from its enforcement responsibilities. In order to encourage voluntary compliance, employers who seek information or assistance from the EEOC will not be subject to any enforcement action.

STATE GOVERNORS' COMMITTEES ON EMPLOYMENT OF THE DISABLED

All states have created their own committees whose mission is to assist and encourage the hiring of people with disabilities, and make sure disabled individuals have an equal opportunity in competing for employment. These committees provide employers with information on hiring disabled workers, and provide disabled workers with resources and contacts to assist them in finding employment.

A directory of state governor's committees on employment of the disabled is set forth in Appendix 8.

CHAPTER 3:
TITLE II - PUBLIC SERVICES

IN GENERAL

Title II of the ADA applies to all state and local governments, their departments and agencies, and any other instrumentalities or special purpose districts of state or local governments. Title II prohibits discrimination against qualified individuals with disabilities in all programs, activities, and services of public entities, including those conducted by state legislatures and courts, town meetings, police and fire departments, motor vehicle licensing, and employment.

Title II also clarifies the requirements of section 504 of the Rehabilitation Act of 1973 for public transportation systems that receive Federal financial assistance, and extends coverage to all public entities that provide public transportation, whether or not they receive Federal financial assistance. It establishes detailed standards for the operation of public transit systems, including commuter and intercity rail (AMTRAK).

Public transportation services operated by state and local governments are covered by regulations of the Department of Transportation, which establish specific requirements for transportation vehicles and facilities. Public transportation services must comply with requirements for accessibility in newly purchased vehicles, make good faith efforts to purchase or lease accessible buses, remanufacture buses in an accessible manner and—unless it would result in an undue burden—provide paratransit in areas where fixed-route bus or rail systems operate.

Paratransit is a service provided to disabled individuals who cannot use regular transit systems independently. Those individuals are picked up and dropped off at their destinations.

REQUIREMENTS UNDER TITLE II

In carrying out the requirements under Title II of the ADA, state and local governments must comply with the following:

1. They are prohibited from denying a disabled person the right to participate in a service, program, or activity simply because the person has a disability. For example, a municipality may not exclude individuals who use wheelchairs from accessing public parks and recreational facilities.

2. They must provide programs and services in an integrated setting, unless separate or different measures are necessary to ensure equal opportunity.

3. They must eliminate unnecessary eligibility standards or rules that deny individuals with disabilities an equal opportunity to enjoy their services, programs or activities unless "necessary" for the provisions of the service, program or activity. For example, requirements that tend to screen out individuals with disabilities, even if not intentional, are prohibited. Nevertheless, safety requirements that are necessary for the safe operation of a particular program may be imposed if they are based on actual risks and not on mere speculation, stereotypes, or generalizations about individuals with disabilities.

4. They are required to make reasonable modifications in policies, practices, and procedures that deny equal access to individuals with disabilities, unless a fundamental alteration in the program would result. For example, a state court building that prohibits animals may modify this policy to allow a sight-impaired person to bring a guide dog into the building.

5. They must provide auxiliary aids and services when necessary to ensure effective communication, unless an undue burden or fundamental alteration would result.

6. They may not assess special charges on individuals with disabilities to cover the costs of measures necessary to ensure nondiscriminatory treatment.

7. They must operate their programs so that, when viewed in their entirety, they are readily accessible to and usable by individuals with disabilities.

Of course, state and local governments may provide additional benefits to the disabled beyond what is required under the ADA.

QUALIFIED INDIVIDUAL WITH DISABILITIES

Title II provides protection to "qualified" individuals with disabilities. For purposes of Title II, an individual is deemed "qualified" if he or she meets the essential eligibility requirements for the program or activity offered by the public entity. The "essential eligibility requirements" will necessarily change depending on the type of service or activity involved.

For example, for some activities it may be essential for the individual to meet specific skill and performance requirements, while for other activities, the essential eligibility requirements would be minimal.

ACCESSIBILITY REQUIREMENTS

Under Title II, state and local governments are required to ensure that disabled persons are not excluded from services, programs, and activities simply because the facilities are inaccessible. This does not mean that they must remove all physical barriers that may prevent access to the disabled. However, they must make their programs accessible to disabled individuals who cannot gain access to the facility due to the nature of their disability. This may be accomplished by relocating a particular program or service to a more accessible facility, or to the individual's home, if feasible.

EXAMPLE: A municipality offers a "free lunch" program to low-income individuals. However, the program operates out of the basement of a municipal building that is not accessible by wheelchair due to a steep flight of stairs. The municipality may comply with the statute by setting aside some additional dining space on the main level of the building, or by home delivery.

Nevertheless, public entities are not required to take any action that would result in a fundamental alteration in the nature of the service, program, or activity, or in undue financial and administrative burdens. This determination can only be made by the head of the public entity or his or her designee and must be accompanied by a written statement of the reasons for reaching that conclusion.

The determination that undue burdens would result must be based on all resources available for use in the program. If an action would result in a fundamental alteration or undue burden, the public entity must take other actions that would not result in such an alteration or burden, but would nevertheless ensure that individuals with disabilities receive the benefits and services of the program or activity.

New Construction and Alterations

Although the Act does not require public entities to rid existing buildings of access barriers, it does establish a high standard of accessibility for new construction and alterations to existing facilities.

Public entities must ensure that newly constructed buildings and facilities are free of architectural and communication barriers that restrict access or use by the disabled. In addition, if a public entity undertakes alterations to an existing building, any altered portions must also be accessible.

Accessibility Standards

Public entities may choose between two technical standards for accessible design:

1. The Uniform Federal Accessibility Standard ("UFAS") established under the Architectural Barriers Act; or

2. The Americans with Disability Act Accessibility Guidelines ("ADAAG"), adopted by the Department of Justice for places of public accommodation under Title III of the ADA.

If the ADAAG standards are chosen, public entities are not entitled to the elevator exemption, which permits certain privately-owned buildings under three stories or under 3,000 square feet per floor to be constructed without an elevator.

The Department of Justice intends to eliminate this choice by amending its current Title III ADA Standards for Accessible Design, which incorporate the ADAAG standards, to add sections dealing with judicial, legislative, and regulatory facilities, detention and correctional facilities, residential housing, and public rights-of-way. The proposed amendment would apply to new construction and alterations under Title II of the ADA.

Funding

Funding is available through the Community Development Block Grant ("CDBG") program at the U.S. Department of Housing and Urban Development ("HUD") for the purpose of taking measures to facilitate access by the disabled, such as installation of ramps, curb cuts, wider doorways, wider parking spaces, and elevators. Governmental entities that have specific questions concerning the use of CDBG funds for the removal of barriers should contact their local HUD Office of Community Planning and Development for additional information.

INTEGRATED PROGRAMS

Title II requires the integration of disabled individuals into the mainstream of society. Thus, public entities may not provide services or benefits to the disabled that are separate or different, unless such separate programs are necessary to ensure that the benefits and services are equally effective. Even in instances when separate programs are permitted, a disabled person still has the right to choose to participate in the regular program.

In addition, state and local governments may not require a disabled individual to accept a special accommodation or benefit if he or she does not want to accept it.

EMPLOYMENT

In addition to the prohibitions against employment discrimination by certain public entities set forth in Title I of the ADA, Title II prohibits all public entities, regardless of the size of their workforce, from discriminating in employment against qualified individuals with disabilities.

COMMUNICATIONS

Under Title II, state and local governments are required to ensure effective communication with individuals with disabilities and, where necessary, must provide appropriate auxiliary aids, without charge. However, public entities are not required to provide auxiliary aids that would result in a fundamental alteration in the nature of a service, program, or activity or in undue financial and administrative burdens.

Types of Auxiliary Aids

The type of auxiliary aid or service necessary to ensure effective communication will vary depending on the length and complexity of the communication involved. For example, a minor service would be for employees to read written instructions to sight impaired individuals. Activities involving more extensive communication, however, may require additional aids or services.

Auxiliary aids and services may include but are not limited to:

1. Sign language interpreters;

2. Magnifying lenses;

3. Readers;

4. Audio recordings;

5. Materials encoded in braille format;

6. Large print materials;

7. Assistance in locating and retrieving items;

8. Assistive listening headsets;

9. Television captioning; and

10. Telecommunications devices—known as TDDs—to assist deaf or mute individuals.

Emergency Telephone Services

State and local agencies that provide emergency telephone services must provide "direct access" to individuals with speech or hearing impairments who rely on a TDD or computer modem for telephone communication. Telephone access through a third party or through a relay service does not satisfy the requirement for direct access. Where a public entity provides 911 telephone service, it may not substitute a separate seven-digit telephone line as the sole means for access to 911 services by non-voice users. A public entity may, however, provide a separate seven-digit line for the exclusive use of non-voice callers in addition to providing direct access for such calls to its 911 line.

FILING A COMPLAINT UNDER TITLE II OF THE ADA

In order to enforce the rights and protections under Title II of the ADA, private individuals may bring lawsuits to enforce their rights under Title II and may receive the same remedies as those provided under section 504 of the Rehabilitation Act of 1973, including reasonable attorney's fees. Individuals may also file complaints with one of the eight designated Federal agencies, listed below.

The complaint should be made in writing, and signed by the complainant or an authorized representative. The complaint should contain the complainant's name and address, and describe the public entity's alleged discriminatory action.

There are eight federal agencies designated to handle complaints under Title II of the ADA:

1. The Department of Agriculture - Covers farming and the raising of livestock.

2. The Department of Education - Covers libraries and educational institutions, excluding those in the health services fields.

3. The Department of Health and Human Services - Covers schools of medicine, dentistry, nursing, and other health-related schools;

health care and social service providers and institutions; and pre-school and daycare programs.

4. The Department of Housing and Urban Development - Covers state and local public housing.

5. The Department of Interior - Covers lands and natural resources, including parks and recreation, water and waste management, environmental protection, energy, historic and cultural preservation, and museums.

6. The Department of Justice - Covers public safety, law enforcement and the administration of justice, including courts and correctional institutions; commerce and industry, including banking and finance, consumer protection, and insurance; planning, development, and regulation; state and local government support services; and all other government functions not assigned to other designated agencies.

7. The Department of Labor - Covers labor and the workforce.

8. The Department of Transportation - Covers transportation, including highways, public transportation, non-law enforcement traffic management, automobile licensing and inspection, and driver licensing.

Complaints may also be filed with any federal agency that provides financial assistance to the particular program or service, or with the Department of Justice that will refer the complaint to the appropriate agency.

A sample discrimination complaint form under Title II is set forth in Appendix 9.

CHAPTER 4:
TITLE III - PUBLIC ACCOMMODATIONS AND SERVICES OPERATED BY PRIVATE ENTITIES

IN GENERAL

Title III of the ADA prohibits places of public accommodation from excluding disabled persons thus depriving them of the goods and services offered. A public accommodation is a private entity that owns, operates, leases, or leases to, a place of public accommodation. There are twelve categories of public accommodations for which the ADA has set forth requirements, including restaurants, hotels, movie theaters, medical offices, drugstores, retail stores, museums, libraries, parks, private schools, and day care centers.

Practically all types of private businesses that serve the public are covered under Title III, regardless of size, including both profit and non-profit businesses. However, private clubs and religious organizations are exempt from coverage.

ELIGIBILITY STANDARDS

If a public accommodation issues standards of eligibility for its services which screen out or tend to screen out disabled individuals, even if unintentional, those standards would be illegal. For example, it would be a blatant violation for a retail store to have a rule that excluded all blind persons from entering the premises.

Subtle forms of discrimination are also prohibited. For example, it would also be illegal for a retail store to prohibit a blind person from paying by check because he or she does not have a driver's license to show for identification, or to ban service animals, such as guide dogs, because they have a "no pets" policy.

DIRECT THREAT

The ADA does permit a public accommodation to exclude an individual if he or she poses a direct threat to the health or safety of others that cannot be mitigated by modifying their policies and procedures, or by providing auxiliary aids.

Nevertheless, safety standards promulgated by a public accommodation must be based on objective requirements rather than stereotypes or generalizations about the ability of persons with disabilities to participate in a particular activity.

AUXILIARY AIDS

There are a number of auxiliary aids and services that may be provided to disabled persons to assist them in taking advantage of services provided by public accommodations. Some of the most common auxiliary aids include sign language interpreters, assistive listening devices, readers, notetakers, braille, or large print materials.

The ADA does not require a public accommodation to provide an auxiliary aid that would result in an undue burden or in a fundamental alteration in the nature of the goods or services provided by a public accommodation.

For example, a restaurant may not be required to provide their menus in braille format because it would cause an undue financial burden. However, the restaurant would be required to have an employee read the menu to a blind or sight impaired individual.

The United States of America v. Walt Disney World

This issue arose in two claims filed with the U.S. Department of Justice against Walt Disney World under Title III of the Americans with Disabilities Act.

Responding to claims by hearing-impaired individuals that they were denied effective communication as required by Title III of the ADA, the Department of Justice began an investigation and an ongoing discussion with Walt Disney World.

The parties subsequently entered into a settlement agreement, ensuring effective communication services to deaf or hearing-impaired visitors at Walt Disney World, and agreed to:

1. Continue to provide those auxiliary aids and services necessary for deaf and hearing-impaired individuals to enjoy the programs and services, including (i) captioning; (ii) sign language interpreters; (iii) assistive listening systems; and (iv) written aids;

2. Make interpreting services available at the magic Kingdom, Epcot, and Disney-MGM Studios on a rotating basis;

3. Provide captioning services at various attractions;

4. Continue evaluating and developing technologies or other methods of providing more effective communication for deaf and hearing-impaired guests;

5. Promote the availability of its services for deaf and hearing-impaired individuals in print and other marketing media;

6. Expand the scope and depth of employee training in disability awareness, etiquette, and services available; and

7. Continue to provide a complaint procedure regarding treatment of guests with hearing disabilities.

The text of the settlement agreement between the United States of America and Walt Disney World is set forth in Appendix 10, Settlement Agreement Between The United States of America and Walt Disney World – Auxiliary Aids.

POLICIES AND PRACTICES

Title III of the ADA requires public accommodations to make reasonable modifications to their policies and practices as necessary to make their goods and services available to persons with disabilities, as long as doing so does not fundamentally alter the nature of their goods and services.

The United States of America v. Budget Rent a Car Systems, Inc.

This issue arose in two complaints filed with the U.S. Department of Justice against Budget Rent a Car Systems, Inc. under Title III of the Americans with Disabilities Act.

The complaints alleged that Budget violated Title III of the ADA because its policies prohibited persons who are unable to drive due to a disability from renting vehicles even when they were accompanied by licensed drivers.

The parties subsequently entered into a settlement agreement established the right of disabled persons to rent Budget vehicles. Budget agreed to modify its rental policies and procedures as follows:

1. For individuals who are unable to drive due to a physical or mental disability, Budget will not require that the method of payment and driver's license belong to the same individual;

2. All persons who wish to rent must have the capacity to enter into contracts;

3. The authorized driver must present a valid driver's license and meet driver qualification requirements imposed by Budget;

4. A renter does not need to show a valid driver's license;

5. Budget shall waive any "additional driver" charges for one person accompanying a renter with a disability that would otherwise apply, and shall not impose any other surcharge in connection with actions required by this policy;

6. Budget shall make an alternative means of access to contract terms available to those individuals who have a vision impairment or who are otherwise unable to read the rental contract;

7. Budget shall inform all employees of the rental policy, and shall incorporate the policy into appropriate training manuals and programs.

The text of the settlement agreement between the United States of America and Budget Rent a Car Systems is set forth in Appendix 11, Settlement Agreement Between The United States of America and Budget Rent a Car Systems, Inc. - Public Accommodations.

SERVICE ANIMALS

The term "service animal" refers to any animal trained to provide assistance to a disabled person. If an animal meets this definition, it is considered a service animal under the ADA regardless of whether it has been licensed or certified by a state or local government.

A service animal is not a pet. It performs functions and tasks that the disabled individual is unable to perform due to the disability. For example, guide dogs are service animals used by blind or sight-impaired individuals. In addition, there are service animals that assist persons with other kinds of disabilities in their day-to-day activities, such as alerting the deaf or hearing-impaired to sounds; or helping mobility impaired persons to retrieve items.

Under the ADA, places of public accommodation are required to permit disabled persons to bring their service animals onto business premises in whatever areas customers are generally allowed. This includes but is not limited to retail stores, hotels, restaurants, movie theatres, public transportation, and taxicabs.

It may not be readily apparent whether a particular animal is a service animal or a pet. Some service animals may be identified by a special harness or collar, but not all service animals wear them. Some service animals may be licensed or certified.

Nevertheless, if the owner represents that the animal is a service animal, even if there are no papers available to identify it as such, the owner still has the right to be accompanied by the animal. In addition, a business may not impose any additional charges when admitting a service animal into the establishment, even if charges are assessed against pets.

However, if the service animal happens to cause any damage, the business can require the animal's owner to make reimbursement provided such reimbursement would be required from a non-disabled person under similar circumstances. In addition, a service animal that exhibits behavior—e.g. vicious growling—which poses a direct threat to the health or safety of others may be excluded. In some instances, if the service animal is disruptive to the particular type of establishment, it may be excluded. This may occur, for example, if a dog continuously barks during a movie.

The United States of America v. Shoney's Inc.

This issue arose in a complaint filed with the U.S. Department of Justice against Shoney's Inc. under Title III of the Americans with Disabilities Act.

The complainants, an individual with a disability and her husband, allege that they were told to leave the restaurant because they were accompanied by a service animal.

The parties subsequently entered into a settlement agreement established the right of disabled persons to bring service animals into the restaurant. Shoney's agreed to modify its policies and procedures as follows:

1. Shoney agreed to post a notice in a conspicuous place in the restaurant stating that individuals with disabilities and their service animals are welcome in their restaurants;

2. Shoney's agreed to adopt and distribute its revised policy regarding service animals for customers with disabilities to all restaurant employees; and

3. Shoney's agreed to train the restaurant's employees as to their obligations under the ADA with respect to service animals.

The text of the settlement agreement between the United States of America and Shoney's Inc. is set forth in Appendix 12, Settlement Agreement Between The United States of America and Shoney's Inc. – Service Animal.

ARCHITECTURAL BARRIERS

An architectural barrier is a physical feature of a public accommodation that limits or prevents disabled persons from obtaining the goods or services offered, such as aisles that are too narrow to accommodate a wheelchair.

Under Title III, public accommodations are required to remove physical barriers that make it difficult for disabled persons to gain access. To assist businesses in evaluating what barriers need to be removed, the ADA has promulgated standards for accessible design as part of the ADA Title III regulations.

The Architectural Barriers Act

Under the Architectural Barriers Act (42 U.S.C. §§ 4151 et seq.) buildings and facilities that are designed, constructed, or altered with Federal funds, or leased by a Federal agency, must comply with Federal standards for physical accessibility. The ABA requirements are limited to architectural standards in new and altered buildings and in newly leased facilities.

Existing Facilities

Many business facilities were built without considering whether they were accessible to disabled individuals, thus, denying them availability to goods and services. Title III of the ADA attempts to remedy this problem.

Under the law, a business that serves the public must remove any physical barriers if it is "readily achievable" to do so—i.e., "easily accomplishable and able to be carried out without much difficulty or expense." The "readily achievable" requirement is based on the size and resources of the business. Therefore, greater efforts would be expected from larger and more prosperous businesses than would be expected from a smaller business.

The cost of modifying an existing structure may be prohibitive, particularly for small businesses. Therefore, for an existing facility, the ADA requires that accessibility be improved without taking on excessive expenses, employing alternative methods of access to the goods and services.

For example, a relatively inexpensive and "readily achievable" barrier removal would be rearranging furniture so as to create a wider path to facilitate movement by wheelchair bound individuals. More drastic measures, such as the installation of elevators, would not likely be required for an existing facility.

Even if barrier removal is not readily achievable, the public accommodation is still required to take some measures to provide its services to the disabled. For example, a fast food restaurant may be required to provide table service to an individual who is unable to stand in line due to his or her disability.

Further, because barrier removal is an ongoing obligation, businesses are expected to remove more barriers as additional resources become available.

New Construction

The ADA requires that newly constructed facilities, first occupied on or after January 26, 1993, meet or exceed the minimum requirements of the ADA Standards for Accessible Design ("ADA Standards"), to facilitate accessibility by the disabled.

For example, new sports stadiums are subject to a number of requirements to satisfy the accessibility requirements of the ADA. A copy of the guidelines are set forth in Appendix 13.

Altered Facilities

Alterations to facilities, including renovations, made on or after January 26, 1992, must also comply with the ADA Standards. Renovations or modifications are considered alterations when they affect the usability of the space. Covered alterations may be as minor as restriping the parking area, or more complex, such as installing new bathroom facilities. In either case, the ADA Standards must be met in order to comply with the Title III requirements.

Parking

Under the ADA, when public parking is provided, there are specific requirements which must be met concerning designated accessible parking for disabled individuals, provided it is readily achievable to do so. For example, an accessible parking space must have space for the vehicle and an additional space located either to the right or to the left of the space that serves as an access aisle to allow a person using a mobility device—e.g., a wheelchair or walker—to get out of the vehicle.

In addition, a sign with the international symbol of accessibility must be readily visible, and located in front of the parking space. The designated accessible parking spaces should be located closest to the entrance of the business. An accessible route must be provided between the access aisle and the accessible building entrance. This route must have no steps or steeply sloped surfaces and must have a firm, stable, slip-resistant surface.

Van accessible parking spaces must have an access aisle that is at least eight-feet wide and should be designated by a sign with the international symbol and the words "van accessible." There should be a vertical clearance of at least 98 inches on the vehicular route to the space, at the parking space, and along the vehicular route to an exit.

The number of accessible parking spaces to be provided is based on the total number of parking spaces. In facilities that are only required to provide one accessible space, that space must also be a van accessible space. In facilities that provide more than one accessible space, one out of eight of those spaces must be van accessible.

Entrances

Businesses are required to make their entrances accessible to the disabled by providing physical access to public sidewalks, public transportation, or the public parking lot. If one or two steps at the entrance prevent access by a disabled person, the business may install a small ramp to facilitate access. When a ramp is added to provide an accessible entrance, the slope of the ramp should be as shallow as possible.

Businesses that have more than one public entrance must provide at least one accessible entrance, which must remain open during business hours.

When it is not readily achievable to provide an accessible entrance, the goods and services must be provided in some other way, if there is a readily achievable way to do so. For example, a grocery store that has a flight of stairs at the entrance making it impossible for a wheelchair bound individual to gain access may take a telephone order and bring the groceries out to the customer. In any event, if some alternative method of service is available, it must be advertised to the public so that they can take advantage of the service.

Once the problems of making the entrance to the business accessible has been solved, it is important that the inside of the establishment permit disabled customers to get around safely and take advantage of the goods and services offered. Specific requirements for a wide variety of settings are set forth in the ADA Standards for Accessible Design. Examples of some of the accessibility requirements are set forth below.

1. A supermarket must make sure its aisles are wide enough to allow wheelchair movement. The customers must also have a way of selecting merchandise from the shelves. Because it is impractical to

locate all of the shelves at a height that will be readily accessible to certain disabled individuals, employees should be available to assist customers in selecting merchandise. Checkout aisles should also provide a minimum width and be identified by a sign with the international symbol of accessibility mounted over the aisle.

2. Fast food restaurants should have serving counters that do not exceed a maximum height, and the ordering line should provide adequate maneuvering space for a person using a wheelchair to move through the line. If these requirements are not readily achievable, the establishment can provide table service for disabled individuals.

3. Restaurants which provide fixed tables and seating—i.e., they are attached to the wall and floor—must provide a certain percentage of accessible seating arrangements to accommodate disabled individuals, e.g. movable chairs.

LEASED PREMISES

In leased premises, the obligation to remove barriers and/or provide auxiliary aids is incumbent on both the landlord and the tenant. The burden may be shifted between the parties by the terms of the lease, however, both will still remain legally responsible should the other breach his or her agreement.

PRIVATELY-OWNED RESIDENCES

Private homes and apartments are not covered under Title III of the ADA unless a place of public accommodation is located within the private residence. For example, many doctors operate their medical practice in a designated area of their home. In that case, the area of the residence used as a place of public accommodation is subject to the ADA.

BUILDING CODES

Many communities have state or local accessibility codes enforced by local building inspectors. Under Title III, existing building codes remain in effect. When a local accessibility code exists, both the code and the ADA requirements must be followed.

The Attorney General is authorized to certify that a state law, local building code, or similar ordinance that establishes accessibility requirements meets or exceeds the minimum accessibility requirements for public accommodations and commercial facilities under the ADA.

A state or local government may apply for certification of its code or ordinance. The Attorney General can certify a code or ordinance only after prior notice and a public hearing at which interested people, including disabled persons, are provided an opportunity to testify against the certification.

If certification is granted, it is considered rebuttable evidence in a subsequent enforcement proceeding that the state law or local ordinance meets or exceeds the minimum requirements of the ADA, i.e., the construction or alteration met the requirements of the ADA because it was done in compliance with the state or local code that had previously been certified.

TAX BENEFITS

As amended in 1990, the Internal Revenue Code allows a deduction of up to $15,000 per year for expenses associated with the removal of qualified architectural and transportation barriers. The 1990 amendment also permits eligible small businesses to receive a tax credit for certain costs of compliance with the ADA.

An eligible small business is one whose gross receipts do not exceed $1,000,000 or whose workforce does not consist of more than 30 full-time workers. Qualifying businesses may claim a credit of up to 50 percent of eligible access expenditures that exceed $250 but do not exceed $10,250.

Examples of eligible access expenditures include the necessary and reasonable costs of removing architectural, physical, communications, and transportation barriers; providing readers, interpreters, and other auxiliary aids; and acquiring or modifying equipment or devices.

FILING A COMPLAINT UNDER TITLE III OF THE ADA

Any individual who feels that they have suffered discrimination by a public accommodation covered under Title III, can file a complaint with the Department of Justice by sending a letter including the following information.

1. The complainant's name, address and telephone number.

2. The name of the public accommodation that committed the discriminatory act.

3. Details of the discriminatory act, including the nature of the act, the date and time it was committed, and the names of the individuals responsible for committing the discriminatory act.

The letter should be signed and dated, and should include any other information or documentation relevant to the incident.

The letter of complaint should be sent to: The Department of Justice, Disability Rights Division, P.O. Box 66738, Washington, D.C. 20035-6738.

Upon receipt of the complaint, an investigation will be initiated to determine whether a violation of the ADA has occurred, and the proper action to be taken.

In cases of public importance, or where a pattern or practice of discrimination is alleged, the Department of Justice will attempt to negotiate a settlement. In general, larger and more prosperous establishments would be expected to make greater efforts to accommodate the disabled.

If a settlement is not possible, litigation may be pursued if warranted. In such cases, the Attorney General may seek monetary damages and civil penalties. Civil penalties may not exceed $50,000 for a first violation, and $100,000 for subsequent violations. Such actions are taken on behalf of the United States, not on behalf of the individual complainant.

A victim of discrimination may also file an individual action in the U.S. District Court. It is not necessary for an individual to file a complaint with the Department of Justice or any other Federal agency, or to receive a "right-to-sue" letter, before proceeding with a lawsuit.

Under Title III, an individual is permitted to allege discrimination based on a reasonable belief that discrimination is about to occur. For example, a disabled individual may have information concerning the plans for new construction of a shopping center. It appears that the design does not call for corridors that are wide enough to be wheelchair accessible. In such a case, it would be less costly and more feasible to require the necessary modifications prior to the start of construction.

CHAPTER 5:
TITLE IV - TELECOMMUNICATIONS

IN GENERAL

Title IV of the ADA amended Title II of the Communications Act of 1934 to provide telephone and television access for people who are hearing or speech impaired. Under Title IV, common carriers—entities providing interstate or intrastate communication by wire or radio as defined in the Communications Act of 1934—such as telephone companies, are required to establish telecommunications relay services on a round-the-clock basis.

TELECOMMUNICATIONS RELAY SERVICES

Telecommunications Relay Services ("TRS") enable hearing or speech impaired callers who use text telephones—known as TDDs or TTYs—and callers who use other devices, such as voice telephones, to communicate with each other through a third party communications assistant.

Many people with hearing or speech disabilities use a TDD instead of a standard telephone. This device employs a keyboard for entering messages and a visual display to view the content of a conversation from another person using a TDD.

To make it easy for people who use a TDD to communicate with businesses and individuals who do not have a TDD, the ADA established a free state-by-state relay network nationwide that handles voice-to-TDD and TDD-to-voice calls. The relay consists of an operator with a TDD who translates TDD and voice messages.

For example, a caller using a TDD calls the relay operator who then calls the intended recipient of the call. The caller types the message into the TDD and the operator reads the message to the recipient. The

---

recipient responds by talking to the operator who then enters the message into the TDD.

The Federal Communications Commission (FCC) has set minimum standards for relay services, and issues regulations specifying standards for the operation of these services. For more information about TRS, contact the FCC as follows:

Federal Communications Commission
445 12th Street SW
Washington, DC 20554
Tel: 888-225-5322 (voice)/888-835-5322 (TTY)
Website: www.fcc.gov/cgb.dro

Speech to Speech Access Services

Speech-to-Speech (STS) is one form of Telecommunications Relay Service (TRS). Like all forms of TRS, STS uses specially trained operators–called Communications Assistants (CAs)–to relay the conversation back and forth between the person with the speech disability and the other party to the call.

Often people with speech disabilities cannot communicate by telephone because the parties they are calling cannot understand their speech. People with cerebral palsy, multiple sclerosis, muscular dystrophy, Parkinson's disease, and those who are coping with limitations from a stroke or traumatic brain injury may have speech disabilities. People who stutter or have had a laryngectomy may also have difficulty being understood. In general, anyone with a speech disability or anyone who wishes to call someone with a speech disability can use STS.

The CAs are specially trained in understanding a variety of speech disorders which enables them to repeat what the caller says in a manner that makes the caller's words clear and understandable to the called party.

A special phone is not needed for STS. You simply call the relay center and indicate you wish to make an STS call. You are then connected to an STS CA who will repeat your spoken words, making the spoken words clear to the other party. The calling party calls the relay center or some other number and asks the CA to call the person with a speech disability. Persons with speech disabilities may also receive STS calls.

A directory of state speech to speech access services is set forth in Appendix 14.

THE TELECOMMUNICATIONS ACT

Sections 255 and 251(a)(2) of the Communications Act of 1934, as amended by the Telecommunications Act of 1996 (47 U.S.C. §§ 255, 251(a)(2)), require manufacturers of telecommunications equipment and providers of telecommunications services to ensure that such equipment and services are accessible to and usable by persons with disabilities, if readily achievable. These amendments ensure that people with disabilities will have access to a broad range of products and services such as telephones, cell phones, pagers, call-waiting, and operator services, that were often inaccessible to many users with disabilities.

CLOSED CAPTIONING

Title IV of the Act requires closed captioning of the verbal content of public service announcements that are produced or funded, in whole or in part, by any agency or instrumentality of the Federal Government.

Nevertheless, under Section IV, a television broadcast station licensee:

1. Is not required to supply closed captioning for any announcement that fails to include the closed captioning; and

2. Is not liable for broadcasting any announcement without transmitting a closed caption unless he or she intentionally fails to transmit the closed caption that was included with the announcement.

FILING A COMPLAINT UNDER TITLE IV OF THE ADA

Title IV is enforced by The Federal Communications Commission, which also enforces the provisions of the Communications Act. If a violation of Title IV is alleged, a complaint should be filed with the Commission. Following its investigation, and within 180 days after the complaint is filed, the Commission issues a final order with respect to the alleged violation.

Intrastate Enforcement

If a complaint to the Commission alleges a violation with respect to intrastate telecommunications relay services within a state, and the state operates a program that is certified by the Commission pursuant to the Communications Act, the Commission directs the complaint to the state for further action.

After the complaint has been referred to the state, the Commission takes no further action unless (i) the state fails to take final action on the complaint (a) within 180 days after it is filed with the state; or (b) within a shorter period as prescribed by the state's own regulations; or (ii) the Commission determines that the state program is no longer qualified for certification.

CHAPTER 6:
TITLE V - MISCELLANEOUS PROVISIONS

IN GENERAL

As its name implies, this section of the Americans with Disabilities Act contains supplemental regulations that are not explicitly covered in other parts of the ADA. Title V is enforced by the U.S. Equal Employment Opportunity Commission (EEOC). Key provisions include those listed below.

ATTORNEY'S FEES

In addition to damages, individuals with disabilities, under the discretion of the judge, can have their attorney's fees awarded as part of the settlement of a successful lawsuit under the ADA.

COVERAGE OF CONGRESS

The House and Senate of Congress, as well as the Judicial branch of the federal government are subject to the ADA. Details on remedies and complaint processing against those entities are explained in this section.

Presently, only the Executive Branch of the federal government claims the right of adhering to Section 504 Rehabilitation Act (1973) guidelines rather than adopt the new ADA guidelines.

EFFECT OF OTHER FEDERAL AND STATE LAWS

This section provides that any other state or federal laws addressing individuals with disabilities can be used under the ADA umbrella. Thus, if a federal or state law provides more stringent protections than those outlined in the ADA, the stricter state or federal provisions can be incorporated into the existing ADA legislation to provide the maximum protection for individuals with disabilities.

ILLEGAL DRUGS AND OTHER EXCLUSIONS

This section states specifically that illegal use of drugs is not a covered disability under the ADA, however it does cover those who were former drug users, with records that show they have participated in rehabilitation programs, or those who are mistakenly regarded as users.

A number of other exclusions from the definition of disability are contained in this section, including kleptomania, compulsive gambling, and pyromania. In addition, the ADA does not protect conditions solely related to sexual identity rather than disability.

INSURANCE UNDERWRITING

The section addressing insurance underwriting practices states that the ADA is not intended to change insurance underwriting practices; however, such practices cannot be used to evade the protections of the ADA.

Thus, employers cannot use this reason to deny a person with disabilities a job because their disability would not be covered or because the cost of insurance would increase. Insurance plans cannot charge different rates, limit coverage available, or refuse to insure individuals unless they can prove their actions are justified by sound actuarial principles or based on actual experience.

MEDIATION

This section provides for the use of alternate means to resolve disputes, including mediation and arbitration. In enacting the ADA, Congress specifically encouraged the use of alternative means of dispute resolution, including mediation, to resolve ADA disputes. In 1994, the Department of Justice established the ADA Mediation Program, which operates under a contract with the Key Bridge Foundation.

Mediation is an informal process where an impartial third party helps disputing parties to find mutually satisfactory solutions to their differences. Mediation can resolve disputes quickly and satisfactorily, without the expense and delay of formal investigation and litigation.

Mediation proceedings are confidential and voluntary for all parties. Mediation typically involves one or more meetings between the disputing parties and the mediator. It may also involve one or more confidential sessions between individual parties and the mediator.

Mediators are not judges. Their role is to manage the process through which parties resolve their conflict, not to decide how the conflict should be resolved. They do this by assuring the fairness of the mediation process, facilitating communication, and maintaining the balance of power between the parties.

Representation by an attorney is permitted, but not required, in mediation. While mediators may not give legal advice or interpret the law, they will refer parties to impartial outside experts within the disability and legal communities when questions or issues needing clarification arise.

A successful mediation results in a binding agreement between the parties. If mediation is unsuccessful and an agreement cannot be reached, parties may still pursue all legal remedies provided under the ADA, including private lawsuits.

Complaints under both Title II (public entities) and Title III (private entities) can be mediated. Disputes involving barrier removal or program accessibility, modification of policies, and effective communication are most appropriate for mediation.

Through its program, the Department refers appropriate ADA disputes to mediators at no cost to the parties. The mediators in the Department of Justice program are professional mediators who have been trained in the legal requirements of the ADA.

Individuals who want to pursue mediation through the Justice Department's program must simply follow the usual procedure for filing a complaint with the Department, and note on the complaint that they want to take the dispute to mediation.

RETALIATION

This provision protects individuals with disabilities who successfully sue a company, government agency, or other entity subject to ADA regulation. It prohibits employers from threatening, intimidating, or retaliating against a person with a disability—or people attempting to aid persons with a disability—for asserting their rights under the ADA. In addition employers are prohibited from threatening, intimidating, coercing, or harassing anyone involved in a successful lawsuit, including those who may have testified on the disabled individual's behalf.

STATE IMMUNITY

In most states, individuals cannot sue state agencies unless these agencies and their affiliated entities agree that they can be sued. This section explicitly provides that states cannot claim immunity from lawsuits brought under the ADA. The ADA ensures that disabled individuals have the right to sue any state agency or affiliated entity that violates its provisions. However, the following case discusses the inability of disabled individuals to recover money damages against the state in such lawsuits.

In *Alabama v. Garrett*, 193 F.3d 1214 (11th Cir. 1999), *reversing* 989 F. Supp. 1409 (N.D. Ala. 1998), the court held that a state employee can sue the state to make that state comply with the ADA but no money damages can be awarded. The court further held that the federal government can sue the state and financial penalties can be assessed.

In this landmark case, the plaintiff sued the University of Alabama's medical center in Birmingham for damages after the institution demoted and then transferred her from her position as a supervising nurse after she was treated for breast cancer. The state argued that Congress lacks the power to require states to pay money damages for injuries caused when states violate the ADA.

The trial judge accepted Alabama's argument, but the U.S. Court of Appeals for the Eleventh Circuit reversed the trial judge's decision. The appellate court found that Congress has the power, under the Fourteenth Amendment to the U.S. Constitution, to require states to pay money damages for violations of the ADA.

The U.S. Supreme Court subsequently agreed to hear the case to resolve a split among the Courts of Appeals on the question whether an individual may sue a State for money damages in federal court under the ADA. In February 2001, the United States Supreme Court ruled 5-4 that suits in federal court by state employees to recover money damages under Title I of the ADA are barred by the Eleventh Amendment (531 U.S. 356 (2001)).

Nevertheless, the majority opinion pointed out that individuals with disabilities still have federal recourse against state employment discrimination: "Title I of the ADA still prescribes standards applicable to the states. Those standards can be enforced by the United States in actions for money damages, as well as by private individuals in actions for injunctive relief ..."

CHAPTER 7:
LAW ENFORCEMENT UNDER THE ADA

ENFORCING THE LAW

In General

Law enforcement personnel often come in contact with disabled persons during the course of their duties. The ADA affects virtually everything that law enforcement officers do, including but not limited to:

1. Processing citizen complaints;

2. Interrogating witnesses; and

3. Arresting, booking, and holding suspects

Unfortunately, actions taken by some disabled individuals may be misconstrued by law enforcement officers as suspicious or illegal.

EXAMPLE: A deaf person may not be able to respond to an officer's questions or directions, and may be perceived as uncooperative.

EXAMPLE: During a routine traffic stop, if an individual has a mobility difficulty, the typical test for intoxication—walking a straight line—will prove ineffective and could lead to false arrest.

EXAMPLE: An individual experiencing a seizure may be perceived as threatening.

Training

To assist law enforcement officers in dealing with situations involving the disabled, law enforcement officers generally receive training in recognizing and handling such situations. For example, officers may be trained to:

1. Identify vehicles that may be driven by a disabled person, including designated license plates or special equipment. In such a case, it would be expected that the driver has some type of disability.

2. Use hand signals to get the attention of a deaf individual.

3. Speak clearly and slowly to make sure that the individual understands what is being said.

4. Administer alternative tests—e.g., the breathalyzer test—to determine intoxication in an individual with a gait disturbance.

Wheelchairs and Mobility Devices

If an individual who uses a wheelchair or other assistive device—e.g., crutches—is taken under arrest, it may be too risky to transport the suspect in the back of the police car as is usually done. Some police departments utilize specially equipped cars or vans to transport disabled individuals. Precaution must be taken to transfer such a person so as to avoid inflicting injury to the individual or damage to the assistive device.

The Visually Impaired

When dealing with an individual who is blind or visually impaired, law enforcement officers must clearly identify themselves. Any documents that the individual is asked to sign must be read and the individual must acknowledge his or her understanding of the content. Prior to taking any action—e.g., fingerprinting—the procedure must be clearly explained so the individual will know what to expect.

Police departments utilize a number of forms that must be completed when a crime is being reported. Blind or visually disabled individuals may be unable to complete such forms. In that instance, most departments have an officer or other employee read the form to the individual and assist in its completion. In cases where the individual has a moderate visual disability, an enlarged reproduction of the form may prove adequate.

The Hearing Impaired

When dealing with a person who is deaf or hearing impaired, law enforcement officers are required to ensure that there is effective communication. This does not automatically require the services of a sign language interpreter every time there is an interaction between the officer and the disabled individual.

For example, some hearing impaired individuals are proficient at lip reading. In such a case, the officer must make sure that he faces the individual directly and enunciates clearly. The parties may also exchange written information. In addition, there are a number of communication aids available to assist deaf or hearing-impaired individuals.

Efforts should be made to provide the disabled individual with the type of aid that he or she is most comfortable with using. However, it is up to the police department to make the final determination provided it is an effective method of communication. Unless it is an emergency situation, officers are advised not to rely on family members for interpreting because they are often too emotionally involved to accurately communicate.

A sign language interpreter may be preferable during interrogations and arrests, in order to ensure effective communication with the individual. This is particularly so, for example, if the legality of the communication may be questioned in court, e.g., whether the individual was "read" his rights.

Most police departments contract with agencies that provide sign language interpreters who are knowledgeable in law enforcement "language." Communication through an interpreter who is not familiar with law enforcement terminology would be ineffective.

The United States of America v. The City of Glendale Arizona Police Department

This issue arose in a complaint filed with the U.S. Department of Justice against the City of Glendale Arizona Police Department under Title II of the Americans with Disabilities Act. The complaint alleged that when the Glendale police officers arrested an individual who was deaf and used sign language for communication, he requested a sign language interpreter, but no interpreter was provided.

The parties entered into a settlement agreement regarding the provision of qualified interpreting services to ensure effective communication with individuals who are deaf or hard of hearing in various police situations. The Glendale Police Department agreed to:

1. Furnish appropriate auxiliary aids and services (including qualified interpreters, written materials, and note pad and pen) when necessary to afford an individual with a disability an equal opportunity to participate in the Police Department's services, programs, or activities;

2. Give the individual the opportunity to request the auxiliary aid or service of his or her choice, and give primary consideration to the expressed choice of the individual, unless the Police Department can demonstrate that another equally effective means of communication is available, or that use of the means chosen would result in a fundamental alteration in the service, program, or activity or in undue financial and administrative burdens;

3. Incorporate a provision in its training program guidelines that, in those situations where interpreting services are necessary to ensure effective communication, the Police Department will secure such services;

4. To instruct all of its employees who are in any way responsible for the provision of appropriate auxiliary aids and services, including qualified interpreters, to comply with the provisions of the settlement agreement; and

5. Conduct a training seminar for current personnel to address the practical application of the ADA to police situations.

The text of the settlement agreement between the United States of America and the Glendale Police Department is set forth in Appendix 15, Settlement Agreement Between The United States of America and Glendale, AZ Police Department – Hearing Impaired Suspect.

Telecommunications Devices for the Deaf (TDD)

A telecommunications device for the deaf (TDD) is an auxiliary aid used by individuals with hearing or speech impairments to communicate on the telephone.

Arrestees who are deaf or hard of hearing, or who are mute or have speech disabilities, may require a TDD for making outgoing calls. TDDs must be available to inmates with disabilities under the same terms and conditions as telephone privileges are offered to all inmates, and information indicating the availability of the TDD should be provided to the arrestee.

Architectural Concerns

Although the ADA requires that the disabled have equal access to law enforcement, it does not require all existing police facilities to be accessible to the disabled. Police departments are not required to undertake alterations that would impose undue financial and administrative burdens. However, there must be some alternative means of access.

For example, a police officer may be dispatched to visit the individual instead of requiring him or her to visit the station. In addition, alternate locations that are accessible may be utilized for the purpose of meeting with disabled individuals.

As it relates to disabled arrestees, the ADA requires that the disabled individual have access to toilet facilities and other amenities provided at the jail. A law enforcement agency is required to make structural changes, if necessary, or arrange to use a nearby accessible facility.

Interrogation rooms should also be accessible for use by arrestees, family members, or legal counsel who have mobility disabilities.

Nevertheless, all new buildings must be made fully accessible to, and usable by, individuals with disabilities. The ADA provides architectural standards that specify what must be done to create access. Unlike modifications of existing facilities, there is no undue burden limitation for new construction. In addition, if an agency alters an existing facility for any reason, the altered areas must be made accessible to individuals with disabilities.

Modification of Police Department Practices and Procedures

Under the ADA, police departments are required to modify their procedures in order to ensure accessibility for individuals with disabilities, unless making such modifications would fundamentally alter the program or service involved. For example, a diabetic prisoner may require sugar to maintain an appropriate blood sugar level. The department may modify the prisoner's meal schedule in order to accommodate his needs.

EMPLOYMENT IN LAW ENFORCEMENT

In General

The ADA guarantees equal opportunity in employment for qualified individuals with disabilities. Nevertheless, the person must also be able to perform the "essential" functions of the position either with or without reasonable accommodation. This is particularly critical for law enforcement officers who are entrusted with safeguarding the health and safety of the public.

Medical Examinations—Job Applicants

Under the ADA, it is illegal to make disability-related inquiries, or give applicants for police employment a medical examination, until a conditional offer of employment is made. This is because disabled applicants were historically denied employment if their disability was discovered.

Nevertheless, if an individual has a "known" disability that would reasonably appear to interfere with or prevent performance of job functions, that person may be asked to demonstrate how these functions will be performed, even if other applicants are not asked to do so. For example, an individual with a hand disability may be asked to demonstrate how he or she would be able to pull the trigger on a gun.

In addition, there is no prohibition against a police department giving an applicant a test that measures his or her ability—e.g. physical fitness tests—before an offer of employment is made. Tests that measure an applicant's ability to perform a task are not considered to be medical examinations. However, the test must be job-related to be legitimate.

Further, the ADA's prohibition on medical exams does not make it illegal for a police department to ask an applicant to provide a certification from a doctor that he or she can safely perform a physical fitness test. The ADA allows an employer to require a limited medical certification in these circumstances. The medical certification should only indicate whether or not the individual can safely perform the test and should not contain any medical information or explanation.

The police department may also ask the applicant to sign a waiver releasing the employer from liability for injuries sustained during the test resulting from any physical or mental disorders.

The ADA does permit police departments to make conditional job offers to a pool of applicants that is larger than the number of currently available vacancies if an employer can demonstrate that, for legitimate reasons, it must provide a certain number of offers to fill current or anticipated vacancies.

However, a police department must comply with the ADA when taking individuals out of the pool to fill actual vacancies, and must notify an individual if his or her placement into an actual vacancy is in any way adversely affected by the results of a post-offer medical examination or disability-related question.

Drug Addiction

Individuals who currently engage in the illegal use of drugs are specifically excluded from the definition of an "individual with a disability." Only individuals who are addicted to drugs, have a history of addiction, or who are regarded as being addicted have an impairment under the law.

In order for an individual's drug addiction to be considered a disability under the ADA, it would have to pose a substantial limitation on one or more major life activities. In addition, the individual could not currently be using illegal drugs.

Denying employment to job applicants because of a history of casual drug use would not raise ADA concerns. However, policies that screen out applicants because of a history of addiction or treatment for addiction must be carefully scrutinized to ensure that the policies are job-related and consistent with business necessity.

If safety is asserted as a justification for such a policy, then the employer must be able to show that individuals excluded because of a history of drug addiction or treatment would pose a direct threat—i.e., a significant risk of substantial harm—to the health or safety of the individual or others that cannot be eliminated or reduced by reasonable accommodation.

It does not violate the ADA to ask whether the applicant has ever used illegal drugs or been arrested for such use. However, a law enforcement agency may not ask at the pre-offer stage about the frequency of past illegal drug use or whether the applicant has ever been addicted to drugs or undergone treatment for addiction.

Nevertheless, under police department standards that disqualify all applicants with felony convictions, it would not be a violation of the ADA to disqualify a former addict with a felony drug conviction, as long as the exclusion is job-related and consistent with business necessity.

Police departments may; however, subject current employees to testing for illegal use of drugs and may require job applicants to undergo such testing at any stage of the application process. Inquiries into the use of prescription drugs are permitted in response to a positive drug test, even though the answers may disclose information about a disability.

Alcohol Addiction

Although a current illegal user of drugs is not protected by the ADA, a person who currently uses alcohol is not automatically denied protection. An alcoholic is a person with a disability and is protected by the ADA if he or she is qualified to perform the essential functions of the job. An employer may be required to provide an accommodation to an alcoholic.

Nevertheless, an employer can discipline, discharge or deny employment to an alcoholic whose use of alcohol adversely affects job performance or conduct. An employer also may prohibit the use of alcohol in the workplace and can require that employees not be under the influence of alcohol during work hours.

Polygraph Tests

Police departments are permitted to conduct polygraph tests before a conditional job offer is made. However, employers must exercise care not to ask any prohibited disability-related inquiries in administering the pre-employment offer polygraph exam.

Background Checks

In general, a job offer is not viewed as "bona fide" under the ADA, unless an employer has evaluated all relevant non-medical information that, from a practical and legal perspective, could reasonably have been analyzed prior to extending the offer.

Nevertheless, a law enforcement employer may be able to demonstrate that a proper background check for law enforcement personnel could not, from a practical perspective, be performed pre-offer because of the need to consult medical records and personnel as part of the security clearance process.

Where the police department uses the information from the medical exam during the background check, doing the background check at the post-offer stage saves the police department the cost of doing a second background check.

Situations in which a police department withdraws an offer after a post-offer background examination will be carefully scrutinized to determine whether the withdrawal was based on non-medical information in the background check or on information obtained through post-offer medical examinations and disability-related inquiries.

If it is determined that the offer was withdrawn because of the applicant's disability, then the police department must demonstrate that the reasons for the withdrawal are job-related and consistent with business necessity.

Medical Examinations—Current Employees

If a current employee becomes injured or ill, a police department can require the employee to take a medical examination provided the examination is job-related and consistent with business necessity.

If, because of the injury or illness, the employee can no longer perform the essential functions of the job, even with reasonable accommodations, the ADA does not require an employer to create a job for the disabled employee. However, the employee must be reassigned to a vacant position for which the individual is qualified if it does not involve a promotion and it would not result in an undue hardship.

A police department may also create a specific class of light duty jobs that are limited to current police officer employees, and which are not available to job applicants, without violating the ADA. Nevertheless, if the employee can still perform the essential functions of his or her job, with or without reasonable accommodation, and without being a direct threat to health or safety, he or she cannot be forced into a light duty position because of a disability.

TELEPHONE EMERGENCY SERVICES

In General

Telephone emergency services refers to basic emergency services—e.g., police, fire, and ambulance—that are provided by public safety agencies, including the "911" system.

Direct Access

Under the ADA, public safety agencies that provide telephone emergency services must provide "direct access" to individuals who use telecommunications devices for the deaf (TDD) or computer modems for telephone communication. "Direct access" means that telephone emergency services can directly receive calls from TDD and computer modem users without relying on state telephone relay services, which utilize communications assistants who use both a standard telephone and a TDD to type voiced communication to the TDD user and read the typed communication to the voice telephone user.

The applicable Title II regulation at 28 C.F.R. §35.162 states:

> Telephone emergency services, including 911 services, shall provide direct access to individuals who use TDDs and computer modems.

Direct access must be provided to all services included in the system, including services such as emergency poison control information. These agencies must ensure that the services for non-voice calls are as effective as those provided for voice calls. Emergency services that are not provided by public entities are not subject to the requirement for direct access.

The Department of Justice established a performance standard through the mandate for direct access instead of utilizing a minimum standard—e.g., mandating the number of TDDs employed by the agency. Thus, while the regulation does not specify a minimum number of TDDs required, the services to individuals who use TDDs must be as effective as those provided to other telephone users.

Therefore, an agency must provide a sufficient number of TDDs to ensure that all TDD calls are answered directly, and that sufficient equipment is available to continue service in the event of emergency, malfunction, or power failure.

Training

Although a public safety agency may have a sufficient number of TDDs to ensure that the calls are answered directly, they still may not be in compliance with the ADA if they lack personnel sufficiently trained in the use of TDDs. An agency must take all appropriate steps to ensure that the TDDs will be used properly. In order to ensure the proper operation of TDDs and related equipment, as well as the effective processing of TDD calls by call takers, the training program should include:

1. General information about the communication issues regarding individuals who are deaf, hearing impaired, or who have speech impairments;

2. Information about American Sign Language; and

3. Practical instruction on identification and processing of TDD calls, including the handling of relayed calls and the importance of syntax and TDD protocol when responding.

Public Education

Public education is crucial to the effective processing of TDD calls. Providing public education to promote the correct use of telephone emergency services, including "911" services, by persons who use TDDs is strongly encouraged.

Non "911" Service Areas

In areas without "911" services, public safety agencies are still required to provide direct access to their telephone emergency services. The agency may comply by providing two separate lines—one for voice calls, and another for TDD calls—rather than providing direct access for non-voice calls on the line used for voice calls. In that case, the services for TDD calls must be as effective as those offered for voice calls in terms of time response and hours of operation.

In addition, the agency must ensure that the TDD number is publicized as effectively as the voice number, and is displayed as prominently as the voice number wherever telephone emergency numbers are listed.

In areas with "911" services, it is also acceptable to have a dedicated seven-digit TDD line for use exclusively by TDD callers in addition to providing direct access for such calls to the "911" line. Where such a separate line is provided, callers using TDDs or computer modems would have the option of calling either "911" or the seven-digit number. However, where a "911" telephone line is available, a separate seven-digit telephone line may not be substituted as the sole means for TDD users to access "911" services.

CHAPTER 8:
ADDITIONAL DISABILITY LEGISLATION AND PROGRAMS

IN GENERAL

As set forth below, in addition to the ADA, there are a number of other laws aimed at assisting the disabled in asserting their rights in areas not specifically covered by the ADA. There are also federal committees, programs and initiatives in place to assist the disabled in crucial areas, such as obtaining employment.

THE AIR CARRIER ACCESS ACT

The Air Carrier Access Act (49 U.S.C. § 41705) prohibits discrimination in air transportation by air carriers against qualified individuals with physical or mental impairments. It applies only to air carriers that provide regularly scheduled services for hire to the public.

Requirements under the Act address a wide range of issues including boarding assistance and certain accessibility features in newly built aircraft and new or altered airport facilities. People may enforce rights under the Air Carrier Access Act by filing a complaint with the U.S. Department of Transportation, or by bringing a lawsuit in federal court. For more information or to file a complaint, contact:

Aviation Consumer Protection Division
U.S. Department of Transportation
400 Seventh Street S.W.
Room 4107, C-75
Washington, D.C. 20590
Tel: 202-366-2220 (voice)/202-366-0511 (TTY)
Tel: 800-778-4838 (voice)/800-455-9880 (TTY)
Website: airconsumer.ost.dot.gov

THE CIVIL RIGHTS OF INSTITUTIONALIZED PERSONS ACT

The Civil Rights of Institutionalized Persons Act (42 U.S.C. §§ 1997 et seq.) authorizes the U.S. Attorney General to investigate conditions of confinement at state and local government correctional institutions such as prisons, jails, pretrial detention centers, and juvenile correctional facilities; publicly operated nursing homes; and mental institutions.

The Act's purpose is to allow the Attorney General to uncover and correct widespread deficiencies that seriously jeopardize the health and safety of residents of institutions. The Attorney General does not have authority under CRIPA to investigate isolated incidents or to represent individual institutionalized persons.

The Attorney General may initiate civil lawsuits where there is reasonable cause to believe that conditions are "egregious or flagrant," that they are subjecting residents to "grievous harm," and that they are part of a "pattern or practice" of resistance to residents' full enjoyment of constitutional or Federal rights, including Title II of the ADA and section 504 of the Rehabilitation Act. For more information or to bring a matter to the attention of the Department of Justice, contact:

U.S. Department of Justice
Civil Rights Division
950 Pennsylvania Avenue NW
Special Litigation Section - PHB
Washington, D.C. 20530
Telephone: 877-218-5228 (voice/TTY)
Website: www.usdoj.gov/crt/split

THE FAIR HOUSING AMENDMENTS ACT

The Fair Housing Amendments Act of 1988 (42 U.S.C. §§ 3601 et seq.) prohibits housing discrimination on the basis of race, color, religion, sex, disability, familial status, and national origin. Its coverage includes private housing, housing that receives federal financial assistance, and state and local government housing.

Under the Act, it is unlawful to discriminate in any aspect of selling or renting housing or to deny a dwelling to a buyer or renter because of the disability of that individual, an individual associated with the buyer or renter, or an individual who intends to live in the residence.

Other covered activities include, for example, financing, zoning practices, new construction design, and advertising. The Fair Housing Act requires owners of housing facilities to make reasonable exceptions in their policies and operations to afford people with disabilities equal housing opportunities.

For example, a landlord with a "no pets" policy may be required to grant an exception to this rule and allow an individual who is blind to keep a guide dog—also known as a "service animal"—in the residence.

The Fair Housing Act also requires landlords to allow tenants with disabilities to make reasonable access-related modifications to their private living space, as well as to common use spaces, although the landlord is not required to pay for the changes.

The Act further requires that new multifamily housing with four or more units be designed and built to allow access for persons with disabilities. This includes accessible common use areas, doors that are wide enough for wheelchairs, kitchens and bathrooms that allow a person using a wheelchair to maneuver, and other adaptable features within the units.

Complaints of Fair Housing Act violations may be filed with the U.S. Department of Housing and Urban Development. For more information or to file a complaint, contact:

Office of Program Compliance and Disability Rights
Office of Fair Housing and Equal Opportunity
U.S. Department of Housing and Urban Development
451 7th Street SW, Room 5242
Washington, D.C. 20410
Telephone: 800-669-9777 (voice)/800-927-9275 (TTY)
Website: www.hud.gov/offics/fheo

For questions about the accessibility provisions of the Fair Housing Act, contact Fair Housing FIRST at:

Tel: 888-341-7781 (voice/TTY)
Website: www.fairhousingfirst.org

For publications, contact the Housing and Urban Development Customer Service Center at:

Tel: 800-767-7468 (voice/relay)

Additionally, the Department of Justice can file cases involving a pattern or practice of discrimination. The Fair Housing Act may also be enforced through private lawsuits.

THE INDIVIDUALS WITH DISABILITIES EDUCATION ACT

The Individuals with Disabilities Education Act (20 U.S.C. §§ 1400 et seq.) requires public schools to make available to all eligible children with disabilities a free appropriate public education in the least restrictive environment appropriate to their individual needs. It requires public school systems to develop appropriate Individualized Education Programs (IEPs) for each child.

The specific special education and related services outlined in each IEP reflect the individualized needs of each student. The Act also mandates that particular procedures be followed in the development of the IEP. Each student's IEP must be developed by a team of knowledgeable persons and must be at least reviewed annually.

The team includes the child's teacher; the parents, subject to certain limited exceptions; the child, if determined appropriate; an agency representative who is qualified to provide or supervise the provision of special education; and other individuals at the parents' or agency's discretion.

If parents disagree with the proposed IEP, they can request a due process hearing and a review from the state educational agency if applicable in that state. They also can appeal the state agency's decision to state or federal court. For more information, contact:

Office of Special Education and Rehabilitative Services
U.S. Department of Education
400 Maryland Avenue SW
Washington, D.C. 20202-7100
Telephone: 202-245-7468 (voice/TTY)
Website: www.ed.gov/about/officees/list/osers/osep

THE NATIONAL VOTER REGISTRATION ACT

The National Voter Registration Act of 1993 (42 U.S.C. §§ 1973gg et seq.), also known as the "Motor Voter Act," makes it easier for all Americans to exercise their fundamental right to vote. One of the basic purposes of the Act is to increase the historically low registration rates of minorities and persons with disabilities that have resulted from discrimination.

The Motor Voter Act requires all offices of state-funded programs that are primarily engaged in providing services to persons with disabilities to provide all program applicants with voter registration forms, to assist them in completing the forms, and to transmit completed forms to the appropriate state official. For more information, contact:

U.S. Department of Justice
Civil Rights Division
950 Pennsylvania Avenue NW
Voting Section - 1800 G
Washington, D.C. 20530
Telephone: 800-253-3931 (voice/TTY)
Website: www.usdoj.gov/crt/voting

THE REHABILITATION ACT OF 1973

Prior to the passage of the ADA, recourse for disability discrimination was mainly sought under the Rehabilitation Act of 1973. In fact, many of the provisions contained in the ADA are based on the Rehabilitation Act and its implementing regulations.

The Rehabilitation Act prohibits discrimination on the basis of disability in programs conducted by federal agencies, in programs receiving federal financial assistance, in federal employment, and in the employment practices of federal contractors. The standards for determining employment discrimination under the Rehabilitation Act are the same as those used in Title I of the Americans with Disabilities Act.

Section 501

Section 501 of the Rehabilitation Act (29 U.S.C. § 791) requires affirmative action and nondiscrimination in employment by federal agencies of the executive branch. To obtain more information or to file a complaint, employees should contact their agency's Equal Employment Opportunity Office.

Section 503

Section 503 of the Rehabilitation Act (29 U.S.C. § 793) requires affirmative action and prohibits employment discrimination by federal government contractors and subcontractors with contracts of more than $10,000. For more information on section 503, contact:

Office of Federal Contract Compliance Programs
U.S. Department of Labor
200 Constitution Avenue NW, Room C-3325
Washington, D.C. 20210
Telephone: 202-693-0106 (voice/relay)
Website: www.dol.gov/esa/ofccp

Section 504

Section 504 of the Rehabilitation Act (29 U.S.C. § 794) states that "no qualified individual with a disability in the United States shall be excluded from, denied the benefits of, or be subjected to discrimination under" any program or activity that either receives Federal financial assistance or is conducted by any Executive agency or the United States Postal Service.

Each federal agency has its own set of section 504 regulations that apply to its own programs. Agencies that provide federal financial assistance also have section 504 regulations covering entities that receive federal aid. Requirements common to these regulations include reasonable accommodation for employees with disabilities; program accessibility; effective communication with people who have hearing or vision disabilities; and accessible new construction and alterations.

Each agency is responsible for enforcing its own regulations. Section 504 may also be enforced through private lawsuits. It is not necessary to file a complaint with a federal agency or to receive a "right-to-sue" letter before going to court.

For information on how to file 504 complaints with the appropriate agency, contact:

U.S. Department of Justice
Civil Rights Division
950 Pennsylvania Avenue NW
Disability Rights Section - NYAV
Washington, D.C. 20530
Telephone: 800-514-0301 (voice)/800-514-0383 (TTY)
Website: www.ada.gov

Section 508

Section 508 of the Rehabilitation Act (29 U.S.C. § 794d) establishes requirements for electronic and information technology developed, maintained, procured, or used by the Federal government. Section 508 requires Federal electronic and information technology to be accessible to people with disabilities, including employees and members of the public.

An accessible information technology system is one that can be operated in a variety of ways and does not rely on a single sense or ability of the user. For example, a system that provides output only in visual format may not be accessible to people with visual impairments and a system that provides output only in audio format may not be accessible to people who are deaf or hard of hearing. Some individuals with disabilities may need accessibility-related software or peripheral devices in order to use systems that comply with Section 508. For more information on section 508, contact:

U.S. General Services Administration
Center for IT Accommodation (CITA)
1800 F Street NW, Room 1234
Washington, DC 20405-0001
Telephone: 202-501-4906 (voice)/202-501-2010 (TTY)
Website: www.gsa.gov/section508

THE VOTING ACCESSIBILITY FOR THE ELDERLY AND HANDICAPPED ACT

The Voting Accessibility for the Elderly and Handicapped Act of 1984 (42 U.S.C. §§ 1973ee et seq.) generally requires polling places across the United States to be physically accessible to people with disabilities for federal elections. Where no accessible location is available to serve as a polling place, a political subdivision must provide an alternate means of casting a ballot on the day of the election. This law also requires states to make available registration and voting aids for disabled and elderly voters, including information by tele-communications devices for the deaf (TDDs) which are also known as teletypewriters (TTYs). For more information, contact:

U.S. Department of Justice
Civil Rights Division
950 Pennsylvania Avenue NW
Voting Section - 1800 G
Washington, D.C. 20530
Telephone: 800-253-3931 (voice/TTY)

MISCELLANEOUS PROGRAMS

The Workforce Recruitment Program

The Workforce Recruitment Program maintains a database of college students with disabilities. The students are available on a full-time or part-time basis. They come from more than 140 colleges and universities, and include graduate and law students.

Each year, recruiters interview about 1,000 students with disabilities at colleges and university campuses across the nation for listing in the database.

The Business Leadership Network

The Business Leadership Network is a national employer-led program operating in concert with the state Governors' Committees. The BLN engages the leadership and participation of companies throughout the United States to hire qualified job applicants with disabilities.

This program offers employers important disability employment information through a network of companies; the opportunity to provide training and work experience for job seekers with disabilities; and recognition for the best disability employment practices.

The Outreach to Small Business Project

The goal of the Outreach to Small Business Project is to educate small and medium-size businesses about the ADA; the benefits of hiring, retaining and promoting people with disabilities; and the resources available to these businesses.

This project utilizes the expertise of members of the employer subcommittee to develop materials and implement marketing strategies to reach small businesses, trade associations and professional service organizations.

The Cultural Diversity Initiative

The goal of the Cultural Diversity Initiative project is to improve employment opportunities for minority persons with disabilities. Recent U.S. Census Bureau statistics reveal that more than 66% of all African-Americans with disabilities are unemployed. In addition, 85% of all severely disabled African-Americans are not working. More than 59% of Hispanic persons with disabilities are unemployed. Individuals with disabilities who are members of other minority groups are also disproportionately represented among the unemployed.

In cooperation with the U.S. Department of Education's Office of Special Education and Rehabilitation Services (OSERS) and key minority organizations, a significant part of this project includes training minority individuals with disabilities, who in turn will be able to educate others within their respective communities on the ADA, disability employment issues, and how to compete for grants funded under Titles I through VIII of the Rehabilitation Act.

Another aspect of the project involves working with minority organizations to develop strategies for reducing the high unemployment rate of minorities with disabilities.

The High School/High Tech Program

The goal of the High School/High Tech Program is to encourage students at the secondary level, and below, to take the necessary academic preparation and skill training to pursue careers in engineering, science and high technology fields. The program provides paid internships and mentoring for high school students with disabilities.

In cooperation with public and private funding sources, businesses and school districts throughout the United States, High School/High Tech programs are active in many cities across the country.

Promoting Entrepreneurial and Self-Employment Opportunities for People with Disabilities Project

The goal of this project is to identify, on a national level, appropriate resources for planning, training, technical assistance, and capital development for individuals with disabilities who wish to develop their own businesses.

Youth Leadership Forums

Youth Leadership Forums endeavor to assist states in developing youth leadership training for high school students with disabilities.

Statistical Tracking of the Employment of People with Disabilities Project

In an effort to advance the employment of people with disabilities, there must be a method by which statistics in this area are measured. Statistical tracking of the unemployment rates of people with disabilities is the only way to determine if progress is being made. The purpose of this effort, which is being coordinated with the Census Bureau and the Bureau of Labor Statistics, is to develop the country's capability to collect, prepare and distribute this type of information.

The Employment of People with Cognitive Disabilities Project

The purpose of this project is to dispel current stereotypes concerning the employability of persons with cognitive disabilities, and to develop white-collar employment opportunities for these individuals, with the primary focus on people with mental retardation.

The Disabled Veterans Employment Forums

The Subcommittee on Disabled Veterans conducts regional forums to review employment issues facing veterans with disabilities in specific geographic areas. Executive summaries, identifying issues that need to be addressed, are prepared for each forum.

Perspectives on Employment of People with Disabilities in the Federal Sector

This annual conference, which is co-sponsored by 10 federal agencies and chaired by the President's Committee, brings together federal EEO officials and personnel representatives who deal with issues that affect the employment of people with disabilities within the federal government.

The Job Accommodation Network

The Job Accommodation Network (JAN) is an international toll-free consulting service that provides information about job accommodations and the employability of people with functional limitations. JAN is open to the public. Calls are handled by consultants who understand the functional limitations associated with disabilities and who have instant access to comprehensive information about accommodation methods, devices and strategies.

The mission of JAN is to assist in the hiring, retraining, retention or advancement of persons with disabilities by providing accommodation information, and to provide public access information to businesses and services needing to comply with the ADA. JAN is not an employment service, but a job accommodation service. Its services are offered free.

APPENDIX 1:
PERCENT OF PEOPLE AGE 5 TO
20 YEARS OLD WITH A DISABILITY
BY STATE (2006)

STATE	PERCENT	RANK
Alabama	7.9	11
Alaska	6.3	34
Arizona	5.8	41
Arkansas	9.0	4
California	5.0	50
Colorado	5.6	44
Connecticut	5.4	47
Delaware	6.6	30
District of Columbia	8.2	7
Florida	6.4	32
Georgia	5.7	43
Hawaii	5.2	49
Idaho	6.6	30
Illinois	5.6	44
Indiana	7.3	17
Iowa	6.9	24

STATE	PERCENT	RANK
Kansas	7.0	23
Kentucky	9.0	4
Louisiana	8.4	6
Maine	10.0	1
Maryland	6.2	36
Massachusetts	7.1	22
Michigan	7.7	12
Minnesota	6.3	34
Mississippi	8.1	8
Missouri	7.3	17
Montana	7.3	17
Nebraska	6.2	36
Nevada	4.0	51
New Hampshire	7.6	13
New Jersey	5.4	47
New Mexico	6.4	32
New York	6.2	36
North Carolina	7.4	15
North Dakota	6.2	36
Ohio	7.5	14
Oklahoma	8.0	10
Oregon	6.9	24
Pennsylvania	7.3	17
Rhode Island	8.1	8
South Carolina	6.7	29
South Dakota	5.5	46
Tennessee	7.4	15
Texas	6.8	27
Utah	5.8	41

STATE	PERCENT	RANK
Vermont	9.5	2
Virginia	6.2	36
Washington	6.9	24
West Virginia	9.2	3
Wisconsin	6.8	27
Wyoming	7.2	21
United States	6.5	

SOURCE: U.S. Census bureau (2006)

APPENDIX 2:
PERCENT OF PEOPLE AGE 21 TO 64 YEARS OLD WITH A DISABILITY BY STATE (2006)

STATE	PERCENT	RANK
Alabama	18.6	5
Alaska	15.0	13
Arizona	12.0	31
Arkansas	20.0	4
California	11.0	41
Colorado	10.9	44
Connecticut	10.6	46
Delaware	13.3	26
District of Columbia	11.3	36
Florida	13.0	28
Georgia	13.1	27
Hawaii	10.1	50
Idaho	13.4	23
Illinois	10.4	49
Indiana	13.4	23
Iowa	11.8	32

STATE	PERCENT	RANK
Kansas	12.4	30
Kentucky	20.2	3
Louisiana	16.9	9
Maine	17.6	7
Maryland	10.6	46
Massachusetts	11.2	38
Michigan	14.1	20
Minnesota	10.5	48
Mississippi	20.5	2
Missouri	15.0	13
Montana	15.4	11
Nebraska	11.3	36
Nevada	11.0	41
New Hampshire	11.7	33
New Jersey	9.7	51
New Mexico	15.0	13
New York	11.5	35
North Carolina	15.1	12
North Dakota	10.8	45
Ohio	14.2	19
Oklahoma	18.1	6
Oregon	14.5	16
Pennsylvania	13.7	22
Rhode Island	13.4	23
South Carolina	15.8	10
South Dakota	11.0	41
Tennessee	17.4	8
Texas	12.7	29
Utah	11.2	38

Americans With Disabilities Act

STATE	PERCENT	RANK
Vermont	14.4	17
Virginia	11.6	34
Washington	14.3	18
West Virginia	21.9	1
Wisconsin	11.2	38
Wyoming	13.8	21
United States	**13.0**	

SOURCE: U.S. Census Bureau (2006)

APPENDIX 3:
PERCENT OF PEOPLE AGE 65 YEARS
AND OVER WITH A DISABILITY
BY STATE (2006)

STATE	PERCENT	RANK
Alabama	48.4	3
Alaska	47.9	6
Arizona	38.9	33
Arkansas	50.5	2
California	41.1	20
Colorado	38.3	39
Connecticut	36.3	48
Delaware	38.8	35
District of Columbia	37.6	45
Florida	38.4	38
Georgia	45.1	11
Hawaii	38.2	40
Idaho	41.4	19
Illinois	39.6	29
Indiana	41.8	18
Iowa	36.0	49

STATE	PERCENT	RANK
Kansas	40.5	24
Kentucky	47.9	6
Louisiana	48.1	4
Maine	40.6	23
Maryland	37.7	43
Massachusetts	37.7	43
Michigan	40.2	25
Minnesota	34.8	51
Mississippi	52.0	1
Missouri	43.3	14
Montana	42.1	16
Nebraska	37.3	46
Nevada	38.7	36
New Hampshire	37.9	42
New Jersey	36.5	47
New Mexico	43.1	15
New York	38.7	36
North Carolina	43.5	13
North Dakota	40.1	26
Ohio	39.8	28
Oklahoma	46.8	8
Oregon	41.0	21
Pennsylvania	39.3	32
Rhode Island	39.4	31
South Carolina	43.7	12
South Dakota	38.1	41
Tennessee	46.0	9
Texas	45.5	10
Utah	38.9	33

Americans With Disabilities Act

STATE	PERCENT	RANK
Vermont	39.9	27
Virginia	39.5	30
Washington	41.9	17
West Virginia	48.1	4
Wisconsin	35.7	50
Wyoming	40.9	22
United States	**41.0**	

SOURCE: U.S. Census Bureau (2006)

APPENDIX 4:
SELECTED PROVISIONS OF THE AMERICANS WITH DISABILITIES ACT OF 1990

TITLE 42 - THE PUBLIC HEALTH AND WELFARE

CHAPTER 126 - EQUAL OPPORTUNITY FOR INDIVIDUALS WITH DISABILITIES

SEC. 12101. FINDINGS AND PURPOSES [Section 2]

(a) Findings. The Congress finds that

(1) some 43,000,000 Americans have one or more physical or mental disabilities, and this number is increasing as the population as a whole is growing older;

(2) historically, society has tended to isolate and segregate individuals with disabilities, and, despite some improvements, such forms of discrimination against individuals with disabilities continue to be a serious and pervasive social problem;

(3) discrimination against individuals with disabilities persists in such critical areas as employment, housing, public accommodations, education, transportation, communication, recreation, institutionalization, health services, voting, and access to public services;

(4) unlike individuals who have experienced discrimination on the basis of race, color, sex, national origin, religion, or age, individuals who have experienced discrimination on the basis of disability have often had no legal recourse to redress such discrimination;

(5) individuals with disabilities continually encounter various forms of discrimination, including outright intentional exclusion, the discriminatory effects of architectural, transportation, and communication

barriers, overprotective rules and policies, failure to make modifications to existing facilities and practices, exclusionary qualification standards and criteria, segregation, and relegation to lesser services, programs, activities, benefits, jobs, or other opportunities;

(6) census data, national polls, and other studies have documented that people with disabilities, as a group, occupy an inferior status in our society, and are severely disadvantaged socially, vocationally, economically, and educationally;

(7) individuals with disabilities are a discrete and insular minority who have been faced with restrictions and limitations, subjected to a history of purposeful unequal treatment, and relegated to a position of political powerlessness in our society, based on characteristics that are beyond the control of such individuals and resulting from stereotypic assumptions not truly indicative of the individual ability of such individuals to participate in, and contribute to, society;

(8) the Nation's proper goals regarding individuals with disabilities are to assure equality of opportunity, full participation, independent living, and economic self-sufficiency for such individuals; and

(9) the continuing existence of unfair and unnecessary discrimination and prejudice denies people with disabilities the opportunity to compete on an equal basis and to pursue those opportunities for which our free society is justifiably famous, and costs the United States billions of dollars in unnecessary expenses resulting from dependency and nonproductivity.

(b) Purpose. It is the purpose of this Act

(1) to provide a clear and comprehensive national mandate for the elimination of discrimination against individuals with disabilities;

(2) to provide clear, strong, consistent, enforceable standards addressing discrimination against individuals with disabilities;

(3) to ensure that the Federal Government plays a central role in enforcing the standards established in this Act on behalf of individuals with disabilities; and

(4) to invoke the sweep of congressional authority, including the power to enforce the fourteenth amendment and to regulate commerce, in order to address the major areas of discrimination faced day-to-day by people with disabilities.

SUBCHAPTER 1 - EMPLOYMENT [TITLE I]

SEC. 12111. DEFINITIONS [SECTION 101]

As used in this title:

(1) Commission. The term Commission means the Equal Employment Opportunity Commission established by section 2000e-4 of this title.

(2) Covered entity. The term covered entity means an employer, employment agency, labor organization, or joint labor-management committee.

(3) Direct threat. The term direct threat means a significant risk to the health or safety of others that cannot be eliminated by reasonable accommodation.

(4) Employee. The term employee means an individual employed by an employer. With respect to employment in a foreign country, such term includes an individual who is a citizen of the United States.

(5) Employer.

(A) In general. The term employer means a person engaged in an industry affecting commerce who has 15 or more employees for each working day in each of 20 or more calendar weeks in the current or preceding calendar year, and any agent of such person, except that, for two years following the effective date of this title, an employer means a person engaged in an industry affecting commerce who has 25 or more employees for each working day in each of 20 or more calendar weeks in the current or preceding year, and any agent of such person.

(B) Exceptions. The term employer does not include

(i) the United States, a corporation wholly owned by the government of the United States, or an Indian tribe; or

(ii) a bona fide private membership club (other than a labor organization) that is exempt from taxation under section 501(c) of the Internal Revenue Code of 1986.

(6) Illegal use of drugs.

(A) In general. The term illegal use of drugs means the use of drugs, the possession or distribution of which is unlawful under the Controlled Substances Act (21 U.S.C. 812). Such term does not include the use of a drug taken under supervision by a licensed health care professional, or other uses authorized by the Controlled Substances Act or other provisions of Federal law.

(B) Drugs. The term drug means a controlled substance, as defined in schedules I through V of section 202 of the Controlled Substances Act.

(7) Person, etc. The terms person, labor organization, employment agency, commerce, and industry affecting commerce, shall have the same meaning given such terms in section 701 of the Civil Rights Act of 1964 (42 U.S.C. 2000e).

(8) Qualified individual with a disability. The term qualified individual with a disability means an individual with a disability who, with or without reasonable accommodation, can perform the essential functions of the employment position that such individual holds or desires. For the purposes of this title, consideration shall be given to the employers judgment as to what functions of a job are essential, and if an employer has prepared a written description before advertising or interviewing applicants for the job, this description shall be considered evidence of the essential functions of the job.

(9) Reasonable accommodation. The term reasonable accommodation may include

(A) making existing facilities used by employees readily accessible to and usable by individuals with disabilities; and

(B) job restructuring, part-time or modified work schedules, reassignment to a vacant position, acquisition or modification of equipment or devices, appropriate adjustment or modifications of examinations, training materials or policies, the provision of qualified readers or interpreters, and other similar accommodations for individuals with disabilities.

(10) Undue hardship.

(A) In general. The term undue hardship means an action requiring significant difficulty or expense, when considered in light of the factors set forth in subparagraph (B).

(B) Factors to be considered. In determining whether an accommodation would impose an undue hardship on a covered entity, factors to be considered include

(i) the nature and cost of the accommodation needed under this Act;

(ii) the overall financial resources of the facility or facilities involved in the provision of the reasonable accommodation; the number of persons employed at such facility; the effect on expenses and resources, or the impact otherwise of such accommodation upon the operation of the facility;

(iii) the overall financial resources of the covered entity; the overall size of the business of a covered entity with respect to the number of its employees; the number, type, and location of its facilities; and

(iv) the type of operation or operations of the covered entity, including the composition, structure, and functions of the workforce of such entity; the geographic separateness, administrative, or fiscal relationship of the facility or facilities in question to the covered entity.

SEC. 12112. DISCRIMINATION [SECTION 102]

(a) General Rule. No covered entity shall discriminate against a qualified individual with a disability because of the disability of such individual in regard to job application procedures, the hiring, advancement, or discharge of employees, employee compensation, job training, and other terms, conditions, and privileges of employment.

(b) Construction. As used in subsection (a), the term discriminate includes

(1) limiting, segregating, or classifying a job applicant or employee in a way that adversely affects the opportunities or status of such applicant or employee because of the disability of such applicant or employee;

(2) participating in a contractual or other arrangement or relationship that has the effect of subjecting a covered entity's qualified applicant or employee with a disability to the discrimination prohibited by this title (such relationship includes a relationship with an employment or referral agency, labor union, an organization providing fringe benefits to an employee of the covered entity, or an organization providing training and apprenticeship programs);

(3) utilizing standards, criteria, or methods of administration

(A) that have the effect of discrimination on the basis of disability;

or

(B) that perpetuate the discrimination of others who are subject to common administrative control;

(4) excluding or otherwise denying equal jobs or benefits to a qualified individual because of the known disability of an individual with whom the qualified individual is known to have a relationship or association;

(5) (A) not making reasonable accommodations to the known physical or mental limitations of an otherwise qualified individual with a disability who is an applicant or employee, unless such covered entity can demonstrate that the accommodation would impose an undue hardship on the operation of the business of such covered entity; or

(B) denying employment opportunities to a job applicant or employee who is an otherwise qualified individual with a disability, if such denial is based on the need of such covered entity to make reasonable accommodation to the physical or mental impairments of the employee or applicant;

(6) using qualification standards, employment tests or other selection criteria that screen out or tend to screen out an individual with a disability or a class of individuals with disabilities unless the standard, test or other selection criteria, as used by the covered entity, is shown to be job-related for the position in question and is consistent with business necessity; and

(7) failing to select and administer tests concerning employment in the most effective manner to ensure that, when such test is administered to a job applicant or employee who has a disability that impairs sensory, manual, or speaking skills, such test results accurately reflect the skills, aptitude, or whatever other factor of such applicant or employee that such test purports to measure, rather than reflecting the impaired sensory, manual, or speaking skills of such employee or applicant (except where such skills are the factors that the test purports to measure).

(c) Covered Entities in Foreign Countries.

(1) In general. It shall not be unlawful under this section for a covered entity to take any action that constitutes discrimination under this section with respect to an employee in a workplace in a foreign country if compliance with this section would cause such covered entity to violate the law of the foreign country in which such workplace is located.

(2) Control of Corporation.

(A) Presumption. If an employer controls a corporation whose place of incorporation is a foreign country, any practice that constitutes discrimination under this section and is engaged in by such corporation shall be presumed to be engaged in by such employer.

(B) Exception. This section shall not apply with respect to the foreign operations of an employer that is a foreign person not controlled by an American employer.

(C) Determination. For purposes of this paragraph, the determination of whether an employer controls a corporation shall be based on -

(i) the interrelation of operations;

(ii) the common management;

(iii) the centralized control of labor relations; and

(iv) the common ownership or financial control of the employer and the corporation.

(d) Medical Examinations and Inquiries.

(1) In general. The prohibition against discrimination as referred to in subsection (a) shall include medical examinations and inquiries.

(2) Preemployment.

(A) Prohibited examination or inquiry. Except as provided in paragraph (3), a covered entity shall not conduct a medical examination or make inquiries of a job applicant as to whether such applicant is an individual with a disability or as to the nature or severity of such disability.

(B) Acceptable inquiry. A covered entity may make preemployment inquiries into the ability of an applicant to perform job-related functions.

(3) Employment entrance examination. A covered entity may require a medical examination after an offer of employment has been made to a job applicant and prior to the commencement of the employment duties of such applicant, and may condition an offer of employment on the results of such examination, if

(A) all entering employees are subjected to such an examination regardless of disability;

(B) information obtained regarding the medical condition or history of the applicant is collected and maintained on separate forms and in separate medical files and is treated as a confidential medical record, except that

(i) supervisors and managers may be informed regarding necessary restrictions on the work or duties of the employee and necessary accommodations;

(ii) first aid and safety personnel may be informed, when appropriate, if the disability might require emergency treatment; and

(iii) government officials investigating compliance with this Act shall be provided relevant information on request; and

(C) the results of such examination are used only in accordance with this title.

(4) Examination and inquiry.

(A) Prohibited examinations and inquiries. A covered entity shall not require a medical examination and shall not make inquiries of an employee as to whether such employee is an individual with a disability or as to the nature or severity of the disability, unless such examination or inquiry is shown to be job-related and consistent with business necessity.

(B) Acceptable examinations and inquiries. A covered entity may conduct voluntary medical examinations, including voluntary medical histories, which are part of an employee health program available to employees at that work site. A covered entity may make inquiries into the ability of an employee to perform job-related functions.

(C) Requirement. Information obtained under subparagraph (B) regarding the medical condition or history of any employee are subject to the requirements of subparagraphs (B) and (C) of paragraph (3).

SEC. 12113. DEFENSES [SECTION 103]

(a) In General. It may be a defense to a charge of discrimination under this Act that an alleged application of qualification standards, tests, or selection criteria that screen out or tend to screen out or otherwise deny a job or benefit to an individual with a disability has been shown to be job-related and consistent with business necessity, and such performance cannot be accomplished by reasonable accommodation, as required under this title.

(b) Qualification Standards. The term qualification standards may include a requirement that an individual shall not pose a direct threat to the health or safety of other individuals in the workplace.

(c) Religious Entities.

(1) In general. This title shall not prohibit a religious corporation, association, educational institution, or society from giving preference in employment to individuals of a particular religion to perform work connected with the carrying on by such corporation, association, educational institution, or society of its activities.

(2) Religious tenets requirement. Under this title, a religious organization may require that all applicants and employees conform to the religious tenets of such organization.

(d) List of Infectious and Communicable Diseases.

(1) In general. The Secretary of Health and Human Services, not later than 6 months after the date of enactment of this Act, shall

(A) review all infectious and communicable diseases which may be transmitted through handling the food supply;

(B) publish a list of infectious and communicable diseases which are transmitted through handling the food supply;

(C) publish the methods by which such diseases are transmitted; and

(D) widely disseminate such information regarding the list of diseases and their modes of transmissibility to the general public.

Such list shall be updated annually.

(2) Applications. In any case in which an individual has an infectious or communicable disease that is transmitted to others through the handling of food, that is included on the list developed by the Secretary of Health and Human Services under paragraph (1), and which cannot be eliminated by reasonable accommodation, a covered entity may refuse to assign or continue to assign such individual to a job involving food handling.

(3) Construction. Nothing in this Act shall be construed to preempt, modify, or amend any State, county, or local law, ordinance, or regulation applicable to food handling which is designed to protect the public health from individuals who pose a significant risk to the health or safety of others, which cannot be eliminated by reasonable accommodation, pursuant to the list of infectious or communicable

diseases and the modes of transmissibility published by the Secretary of Health and Human Services.

SEC. 12114. ILLEGAL USE OF DRUGS AND ALCOHOL [SECTION 103]

(a) Qualified Individual With a Disability. For purposes of this title, the term qualified individual with a disability shall not include any employee or applicant who is currently engaging in the illegal use of drugs, when the covered entity acts on the basis of such use.

(b) Rules of Construction. Nothing in subsection (a) shall be construed to exclude as a qualified individual with a disability an individual who

(1) has successfully completed a supervised drug rehabilitation program and is no longer engaging in the illegal use of drugs, or has otherwise been rehabilitated successfully and is no longer engaging in such use;

(2) is participating in a supervised rehabilitation program and is no longer engaging in such use; or

(3) is erroneously regarded as engaging in such use, but is not engaging in such use; except that it shall not be a violation of this Act for a covered entity to adopt or administer reasonable policies or procedures, including but not limited to drug testing, designed to ensure that an individual described in paragraph (1) or (2) is no longer engaging in the illegal use of drugs.

(c) Authority of Covered Entity. A covered entity

(1) may prohibit the illegal use of drugs and the use of alcohol at the workplace by all employees;

(2) may require that employees shall not be under the influence of alcohol or be engaging in the illegal use of drugs at the workplace;

(3) may require that employees behave in conformance with the requirements established under the Drug-Free Workplace Act of 1988 (41 U.S.C. 701 et seq.);

(4) may hold an employee who engages in the illegal use of drugs or who is an alcoholic to the same qualification standards for employment or job performance and behavior that such entity holds other employees, even if any unsatisfactory performance or behavior is related to the drug use or alcoholism of such employee; and

(5) may, with respect to Federal regulations regarding alcohol and the illegal use of drugs, require that

(A) employees comply with the standards established in such regulations of the Department of Defense, if the employees of the covered entity are employed in an industry subject to such regulations, including complying with regulations (if any) that apply to employment in sensitive positions in such an industry, in the case of employees of the covered entity who are employed in such positions (as defined in the regulations of the Department of Defense);

(B) employees comply with the standards established in such regulations of the Nuclear Regulatory Commission, if the employees of the covered entity are employed in an industry subject to such regulations, including complying with regulations (if any) that apply to employment in sensitive positions in such an industry, in the case of employees of the covered entity who are employed in such positions (as defined in the regulations of the Nuclear Regulatory Commission); and

(C) employees comply with the standards established in such regulations of the Department of Transportation, if the employees of the covered entity are employed in a transportation industry subject to such regulations, including complying with such regulations (if any) that apply to employment in sensitive positions in such an industry, in the case of employees of the covered entity who are employed in such positions (as defined in the regulations of the Department of Transportation).

(d) Drug Testing.

(1) In general. For purposes of this title, a test to determine the illegal use of drugs shall not be considered a medical examination.

(2) Construction. Nothing in this title shall be construed to encourage, prohibit, or authorize the conducting of drug testing for the illegal use of drugs by job applicants or employees or making employment decisions based on such test results.

(e) Transportation Employees. Nothing in this title shall be construed to encourage, prohibit, restrict, or authorize the otherwise lawful exercise by entities subject to the jurisdiction of the Department of Transportation of authority to

(1) test employees of such entities in, and applicants for, positions involving safety-sensitive duties for the illegal use of drugs and for on-duty impairment by alcohol; and

(2) remove such persons who test positive for illegal use of drugs and on-duty impairment by alcohol pursuant to paragraph (1) from safety-sensitive duties in implementing subsection (c).

SEC. 12115. POSTING NOTICES [SECTION 105]

Every employer, employment agency, labor organization, or joint labor-management committee covered under this title shall post notices in an accessible format to applicants, employees, and members describing the applicable provisions of this Act, in the manner prescribed by section 711 of the Civil Rights Act of 1964 (42 U.S.C. 2000e-10).

SEC. 12116. REGULATIONS [SECTION 106]

Not later than 1 year after the date of enactment of this Act, the Commission shall issue regulations in an accessible format to carry out this title in accordance with subchapter II of chapter 5 of title 5, United States Code.

SEC. 12117. ENFORCEMENT [SECTION 107]

(a) Powers, Remedies, and Procedures. The powers, remedies, and procedures set forth in sections 705, 706, 707, 709, and 710 of the Civil Rights Act of 1964 (42 U.S.C. 2000e-4, 2000e-5, 2000e-6, 2000e-8, and 2000e-9) shall be the powers, remedies, and procedures this title provides to the Commission, to the Attorney General, or to any person alleging discrimination on the basis of disability in violation of any provision of this Act, or regulations promulgated under section 106, concerning employment.

(b) Coordination. The agencies with enforcement authority for actions which allege employment discrimination under this title and under the Rehabilitation Act of 1973 shall develop procedures to ensure that administrative complaints filed under this title and under the Rehabilitation Act of 1973 are dealt with in a manner that avoids duplication of effort and prevents imposition of inconsistent or conflicting standards for the same requirements under this title and the Rehabilitation Act of 1973. The Commission, the Attorney General, and the Office of Federal Contract Compliance Programs shall establish such coordinating mechanisms (similar to provisions contained in the joint regulations promulgated by the Commission and the Attorney General at part 42 of title 28 and part 1691 of title 29, Code of Federal Regulations, and the Memorandum of Understanding between the Commission and the Office of Federal Contract Compliance Programs dated January 16, 1981 (46 Fed. Reg. 7435, January 23, 1981)) in regulations implementing this title and Rehabilitation Act of 1973 not later than 18 months after the date of enactment of this Act.

SUBCHAPTER II - PUBLIC SERVICES [TITLE II]

PART A - PROHIBITION AGAINST DISCRIMINATION AND OTHER GENERALLY APPLICABLE PROVISIONS [SUBTITLE A]

SEC. 12131. DEFINITIONS [SECTION 201]

As used in this title:

(1) Public entity. The term public entity means (A) any State or local government; (B) any department, agency, special purpose district, or other instrumentality of a State or States or local government; and (C) the National Railroad Passenger Corporation, and any commuter authority (as defined in section 103(8) of the Rail Passenger Service Act).

(2) Qualified individual with a disability. The term qualified individual with a disability means an individual with a disability who, with or without reasonable modifications to rules, policies, or practices, the removal of architectural, communication, or transportation barriers, or the provision of auxiliary aids and services, meets the essential eligibility requirements for the receipt of services or the participation in programs or activities provided by a public entity.

SEC. 12132. DISCRIMINATION [SECTION 202]

Subject to the provisions of this title, no qualified individual with a disability shall, by reason of such disability, be excluded from participation in or be denied the benefits of the services, programs, or activities of a public entity, or be subjected to discrimination by any such entity.

SEC. 12133. ENFORCEMENT [SECTION 203]

The remedies, procedures, and rights set forth in section 505 of the Rehabilitation Act of 1973 (29 U.S.C. 794a) shall be the remedies, procedures, and rights this title provides to any person alleging discrimination on the basis of disability in violation of section 202.

SEC. 12134. REGULATIONS [SECTION 204]

(a) In General. Not later than 1 year after the date of enactment of this Act, the Attorney General shall promulgate regulations in an accessible format that implement this subtitle. Such regulations shall not include any matter within the scope of the authority of the Secretary of Transportation under section 223, 229, or 244.

(b) Relationship to Other Regulations. Except for program accessibility, existing facilities, and communications, regulations under subsection (a) shall be consistent with this Act and with the coordination regulations under part 41 of title 28, Code of Federal Regulations (as promulgated by the Department of Health, Education, and Welfare on January 13, 1978), applicable to recipients of Federal financial assistance under section 504 of the Rehabilitation Act of 1973 (29 U.S.C. 794). With respect to program accessibility, existing facilities, and communications, such regulations shall be consistent with regulations and analysis as in part 39 of title 28 of the Code of Federal Regulations, applicable to federally conducted activities under such section 504.

(c) Standards. Regulations under subsection (a) shall include standards applicable to facilities and vehicles covered by this subtitle, other than facilities, stations, rail passenger cars, and vehicles covered by subtitle B. Such standards shall be consistent with the minimum guidelines and requirements issued by the Architectural and Transportation Barriers Compliance Board in accordance with section 504(a) of this Act.

PART B - ACTIONS APPLICABLE TO PUBLIC TRANSPORTATION PROVIDED BY PUBLIC ENTITIES CONSIDERED DISCRIMINATORY [SUBTITLE B]

SUBPART I - PUBLIC TRANSPORTATION OTHER THAN BY AIRCRAFT OR CERTAIN RAIL OPERATIONS [PART I]

SEC. 1241. DEFINITIONS [SECTION 221]

As used in this part:

(1) Demand responsive system. The term demand responsive system means any system of providing designated public transportation which is not a fixed route system.

(2) Designated public transportation. The term designated public transportation means transportation (other than public school transportation) by bus, rail, or any other conveyance (other than transportation by aircraft or intercity or commuter rail transportation (as defined in section 241)) that provides the general public with general or special service (including charter service) on a regular and continuing basis.

(3) Fixed route system. The term fixed route system means a system of providing designated public transportation on which a vehicle is operated along a prescribed route according to a fixed schedule.

(4) Operates. The term operates, as used with respect to a fixed route system or demand responsive system, includes operation of such system by a person under a contractual or other arrangement or relationship with a public entity.

(5) Public school transportation. The term public school transportation means transportation by school bus vehicles of schoolchildren, personnel, and equipment to and from a public elementary or secondary school and school-related activities.

(6) Secretary. The term Secretary means the Secretary of Transportation.

SEC. 12142. PUBLIC ENTITIES OPERATING FIXED ROUTE SYSTEMS [SECTION 222]

(a) Purchase and Lease of New Vehicles. It shall be considered discrimination for purposes of section 202 of this Act and section 504 of the Rehabilitation Act of 1973 (29 U.S.C. 794) for a public entity which operates a fixed route system to purchase or lease a new bus, a new rapid rail vehicle, a new light rail vehicle, or any other new vehicle to be used on such system, if the solicitation for such purchase or lease is made after the 30th day following the effective date of this subsection and if such bus, rail vehicle, or other vehicle is not readily accessible to and usable by individuals with disabilities, including individuals who use wheelchairs.

(b) Purchase and Lease of Used Vehicles. Subject to subsection (c)(1), it shall be considered discrimination for purposes of section 202 of this Act and section 504 of the Rehabilitation Act of 1973 (29 U.S.C. 794) for a public entity which operates a fixed route system to purchase or lease, after the 30th day following the effective date of this subsection, a used vehicle for use on such system unless such entity makes demonstrated good faith efforts to purchase or lease a used vehicle for use on such system that is readily accessible to and usable by individuals with disabilities, including individuals who use wheelchairs.

(c) Remanufactured Vehicles.

(1) General rule. Except as provided in paragraph (2), it shall be considered discrimination for purposes of section 202 of this Act and section 504 of the Rehabilitation Act of 1973 (29 U.S.C.794) for a public entity which operates a fixed route system

(A) to remanufacture a vehicle for use on such system so as to extend its usable life for 5 years or more, which remanufacture begins (or for which the solicitation is made) after the 30th day following the effective date of this subsection; or

(B) to purchase or lease for use on such system a remanufactured vehicle which has been remanufactured so as to extend its usable life for 5 years or more, which purchase or lease occurs after such 30th day and during the period in which the usable life is extended; unless, after remanufacture, the vehicle is, to the maximum extent feasible, readily accessible to and usable by individuals with disabilities, including individuals who use wheelchairs.

(2) Exception for historic vehicles.

(A) General rule. If a public entity operates a fixed route system any segment of which is included on the National Register of Historic Places and if making a vehicle of historic character to be used solely on such segment readily accessible to and usable by individuals with disabilities would significantly alter the historic character of such vehicle, the public entity only has to make (or to purchase or lease a remanufactured vehicle with) those modifications which are necessary to meet the requirements of paragraph (1) and which do not significantly alter the historic character of such vehicle.

(B) Vehicles of historic character defined by regulations. For purposes of this paragraph and section 228(b), a vehicle of historic character shall be defined by the regulations issued by the Secretary to carry out this subsection.

SEC. 12143. PARATRANSIT AS A COMPLEMENT TO FIXED ROUTE SERVICE [SECTION 223]

(a) General Rule. It shall be considered discrimination for purposes of section 202 of this Act and section 504 of the Rehabilitation Act of 1973 (29 U.S.C. 794) for a public entity which operates a fixed route system (other than a system which provides solely commuter bus service) to fail to provide with respect to the operations of its fixed route system, in accordance with this section, paratransit and other special transportation services to individuals with disabilities, including individuals who use wheelchairs, that are sufficient to provide to such individuals a level of service (1) which is comparable to the level of designated public transportation services provided to individuals without disabilities using such system; or (2) in the case of response time, which is comparable, to the extent practicable, to the level of designated public transportation services provided to individuals without disabilities using such system.

(b) Issuance of Regulations (Omitted)

(c) Required Contents of Regulations (Omitted)

(d) Review of Plan (Omitted)

(e) Discrimination Defined. As used in subsection (a), the term discrimination includes

(1) a failure of a public entity to which the regulations issued under this section apply to submit, or commence implementation of, a plan in accordance with subsections (c)(6) and (c)(7);

(2) a failure of such entity to submit, or commence implementation of, a modified plan in accordance with subsection (d)(3);

(3) submission to the Secretary of a modified plan under subsection (d)(3) which does not meet the requirements of this section; or

(4) a failure of such entity to provide paratransit or other special transportation services in accordance with the plan or modified plan the public entity submitted to the Secretary under this section.

(f) Statutory Construction (Omitted)

SEC. 12144. PUBLIC ENTITY OPERATING A DEMAND RESPONSIVE SYSTEM [SECTION 224]

If a public entity operates a demand responsive system, it shall be considered discrimination, for purposes of section 202 of this Act and section 504 of the Rehabilitation Act of 1973 (29 U.S.C. 794), for such entity to purchase or lease a new vehicle for use on such system, for which a solicitation is made after the 30th day following the effective date of this section, that is not readily accessible to and usable by individuals with disabilities, including individuals who use wheelchairs, unless such system, when viewed in its entirety, provides a level of service to such individuals equivalent to the level of service such system provides to individuals without disabilities.

SEC. 12145. TEMPORARY RELIEF WHERE LIFTS ARE UNAVAILABLE [SECTION 225](OMITTED)

SEC. 12146. NEW FACILITIES [SECTION 226]

For purposes of section 202 of this Act and section 504 of the Rehabilitation Act of 1973 (29 U.S.C. 794), it shall be considered discrimination for a public entity to construct a new facility to be used in the provision of designated public transportation services unless such facility is readily accessible to and usable by individuals with disabilities, including individuals who use wheelchairs.

SEC. 12147. ALTERATIONS OF EXISTING FACILITIES [SECTION 227]

(a) General Rule. With respect to alterations of an existing facility or part thereof used in the provision of designated public transportation services that affect or could affect the usability of the facility or part thereof, it shall be considered discrimination, for purposes of section 202 of this Act and section 504 of the Rehabilitation Act of 1973 (29 U.S.C. 794), for a public entity to fail to make such alterations (or to ensure that the alterations are made) in such a manner that, to the maximum extent feasible, the altered portions of the facility are readily accessible to and usable by individuals with disabilities, including individuals who use wheelchairs, upon the completion of such alterations. Where the public entity is undertaking an alteration that affects or could affect usability of or access to an area of the facility containing a primary function, the entity shall also make the alterations in such a manner that, to the maximum extent feasible, the path of travel to the altered area and the bathrooms, telephones, and drinking fountains serving the altered area, are readily accessible to and usable by individuals with disabilities, including individuals who use wheelchairs, upon completion of such alterations, where such alterations to the path of travel or the bathrooms, telephones, and drinking fountains serving the altered area are not disproportionate to the overall alterations in terms of cost and scope (as determined under criteria established by the Attorney General).

(b) Special Rule for Stations.

(1) General rule. For purposes of section 202 of this Act and section 504 of the Rehabilitation Act of 1973 (29 U.S.C. 794), it shall be considered discrimination for a public entity that provides designate public transportation to fail, in accordance with the provisions of this subsection, to make key stations (as determined under criteria established by the Secretary by regulation) in rapid rail and light rail systems readily accessible to and usable by individuals with disabilities, including individuals who use wheelchairs.

(2) Rapid rail and light rail key stations (Omitted)

SEC. 12148. PUBLIC TRANSPORTATION PROGRAMS AND ACTIVITIES IN EXISTING FACILITIES AND ONE CAR PER TRAIN RULE [SECTION 228]

(a) Public Transportation Programs and Activities in Existing Facilities.

(1) In general. With respect to existing facilities used in the provision of designated public transportation services, it shall be considered discrimination, for purposes of section 202 of this Act and section 504 of the Rehabilitation Act of 1973 (29 U.S.C. 794), for a public entity to fail to operate a designated public transportation program or activity conducted in such facilities so that, when viewed in the entirety, the program or activity is readily accessible to and usable by individuals with disabilities.

(2) Exception. Paragraph (1) shall not require a public entity to make structural changes to existing facilities in order to make such facilities accessible to individuals who use wheelchairs, unless and to the extent required by section 227(a) (relating to alterations) or section 227(b) (relating to key stations).

(3) Utilization. Paragraph (1) shall not require a public entity to which paragraph (2) applies, to provide to individuals who use wheelchairs services made available to the general public at such facilities when such individuals could not utilize or benefit from such services provided at such facilities.

(b) One Car Per Train Rule.

(1) General rule. Subject to paragraph (2), with respect to 2 or more vehicles operated as a train by a light or rapid rail system, for purposes of section 202 of this Act and section 504 of the Rehabilitation Act of 1973 (29 U.S.C. 794), it shall be considered discrimination for a public entity to fail to have at least 1 vehicle per train that is accessible to individuals with disabilities, including individuals who use wheelchairs, as soon as practicable but in no event later than the last day of the 5-year period beginning on the effective date of this section.

(2) Historic trains. In order to comply with paragraph (1) with respect to the remanufacture of a vehicle of historic character which is to be used on a segment of a light or rapid rail system which is included on the National Register of Historic Places, if making such vehicle readily accessible to and usable by individuals with disabilities would significantly alter the historic character of such vehicle, the public entity which operates such system only has to make (or to purchase or lease a remanufactured vehicle with) those modifications which are necessary to meet the requirements of section 222(c)(1) and which do not significantly alter the historic character of such vehicle.

SEC. 1249. REGULATIONS [SECTION 229] (OMITTED)

SEC. 12150. INTERIM ACCESSIBILITY REQUIREMENTS [SECTION 230] (OMITTED)

SUBPART II - PUBLIC TRANSPORTATION BY INTERCITY AND COMMUTER RAIL [PART II]

SEC. 12161. DEFINITIONS [SECTION 241]

As used in this part:

(1) Commuter authority. The term commuter authority has the meaning given such term in section 103(8) of the Rail Passenger Service Act (45 U.S.C. 502(8)).

(2) Commuter rail transportation. The term commuter rail transportation has the meaning given the term commuter service in section 103(9) of the Rail Passenger Service Act (45 U.S.C. 502(9)).

(3) Intercity rail transportation. The term intercity rail transportation means transportation provided by the National Railroad Passenger Corporation.

(4) Rail passenger car. The term rail passenger car means, with respect to intercity rail transportation, single-level and bi-level coach cars, single-level and bi-level dining cars, single-level and bi-level sleeping cars, single-level and bi-level lounge cars, and food service cars.

(5) Responsible person. The term responsible person means (A) in the case of a station more than 50 percent of which is owned by a public entity, such public entity; (B) in the case of a station more than 50 percent of which is owned by a private party, the persons providing intercity or commuter rail transportation to such station, as allocated on an equitable basis by regulation by the Secretary of Transportation; and (C) in a case where no party owns more than 50 percent of a station, the persons providing intercity or commuter rail transportation to such station and the owners of the station, other than private party owners, as allocated on an equitable basis by regulation by the Secretary of Transportation.

(6) Station. The term station means the portion of a property located appurtenant to a right-of-way on which intercity or commuter rail transportation is operated, where such portion is used by the general public and is related to the provision of such transportation, including passenger platforms, designated waiting areas, ticketing areas, restrooms, and, where a public entity providing rail transportation owns the property, concession areas, to the extent that such public

entity exercises control over the selection, design, construction, or alteration of the property, but such term does not include flag stops.

SEC. 12162. INTERCITY AND COMMUTER RAIL ACTIONS CONSIDERED DISCRIMINATORY [SECTION 242]

(a) Intercity Rail Transportation.

(1) One car per train rule. It shall be considered discrimination for purposes of section 202 of this Act and section 504 of the Rehabilitation Act of 1973 (29 U.S.C. 794) for a person who provides intercity rail transportation to fail to have at least one passenger car per train that is readily accessible to and usable by individuals with disabilities, including individuals who use wheelchairs, in accordance with regulations issued under section 244, as soon as practicable, but in no event later than 5 years after the date of enactment of this Act.

(2) New intercity cars.

(A) General rule. Except as otherwise provided in this subsection with respect to individuals who use wheelchairs, it shall be considered discrimination for purposes of section 202 of this Act and section 504 of the Rehabilitation Act of 1973 (29 U.S.C. 794) for a person to purchase or lease any new rail passenger cars for use in intercity rail transportation, and for which a solicitation is made later than 30 days after the effective date of this section, unless all such rail cars are readily accessible to and usable by individuals with disabilities, including individuals who use wheelchairs, as prescribed by the Secretary of Transportation in regulations issued under section 244.

(B) Special rule for single-level passenger coaches for individuals who use wheelchairs. Single-level passenger coaches shall be required to (i) be able to be entered by an individual who uses a wheelchair; (ii) have space to park and secure a wheelchair; (iii) have a seat to which a passenger in a wheelchair can transfer, and a space to fold and store such passengers wheelchair; and (iv) have a restroom usable by an individual who uses a wheelchair, only to the extent provided in paragraph (3).

(C) Special rule for single-level dining cars for individuals who use wheelchairs. Single-level dining cars shall not be required to (i) be able to be entered from the station platform by an individual who uses a wheelchair; or (ii) have a restroom usable by an individual who uses a wheelchair if no restroom is provided in such car for any passenger.

(D) Special rule for bi-level dining cars for individuals who use wheelchairs. Bi-level dining cars shall not be required to (i) be able to be entered by an individual who uses a wheelchair; (ii) have space to park and secure a wheelchair; (iii) have a seat to which a passenger in a wheelchair can transfer, or a space to fold and store such passengers wheelchair; or (iv) have a restroom usable by an individual who uses a wheelchair.

(3) Accessibility of single-level coaches.

(A) General rule.It shall be considered discrimination for purposes of section 202 of this Act and section 504 of the Rehabilitation Act of 1973 (29 U.S.C. 794) for a person who provides intercity rail transportation to fail to have on each train which includes one or more single-level rail passenger coaches (i) a number of spaces (I) to park and secure wheelchairs (to accommodate individuals who wish to remain in their wheelchairs) equal to not less than one-half of the number of single-level rail passenger coaches in such train; and (II) to fold and store wheelchairs (to accommodate individuals who wish to transfer to coach seats) equal to not less than one-half of the number of single-level rail passenger coaches in such train, as soon as practicable, but in no event later than 5 years after the date of enactment of this Act; and (ii) a number of spaces (I) to park and secure wheelchairs (to accommodate individuals who wish to remain in their wheelchairs) equal to not less than the total number of single-level rail passenger coaches in such train; and (II) to fold and store wheelchairs (to accommodate individuals who wish to transfer to coach seats) equal to not less than the total number of single-level rail passenger coaches in such train, as soon as practicable, but in no event later than 10 years after the date of enactment of this Act.

(B) Location (Omitted)

(C) Limitation (Omitted)

(D) Other accessibility features (Omitted)

(4) Food service (Omitted)

(b) Commuter Rail Transportation.

(1) One car per train rule. It shall be considered discrimination for purposes of section 202 of this Act and section 504 of the

Rehabilitation Act of 1973 (29 U.S.C. 794) for a person who provides commuter rail transportation to fail to have at least one passenger car per train that is readily accessible to and usable by individuals with disabilities, including individuals who use wheelchairs, in accordance with regulations issued under section 244, as soon as practicable, but in no event later than 5 years after the date of enactment of this Act.

(2) New commuter rail cars.

(A) General rule. It shall be considered discrimination for purposes of section 202 of this Act and section 504 of the Rehabilitation Act of 1973 (29 U.S.C. 794) for a person to purchase or lease any new rail passenger cars for use in commuter rail transportation, and for which a solicitation is made later than 30 days after the effective date of this section, unless all such railcars are readily accessible to and usable by individuals with disabilities, including individuals who use wheelchairs, as prescribed by the Secretary of Transportation in regulations issued under section 244.

(B) Accessibility. (Omitted)

(c) Used Rail Cars. It shall be considered discrimination for purposes of section 202 of this Act and section 504 of the Rehabilitation Act of 1973 (29 U.S.C. 794) for a person to purchase or lease a used rail passenger car for use in intercity or commuter rail transportation, unless such person makes demonstrated good faith efforts to purchase or lease a used rail car that is readily accessible to and usable by individuals with disabilities, including individuals who use wheelchairs, as prescribed by the Secretary of Transportation in regulations issued under section 244.

(d) Remanufactured Rail Cars.

(1) Remanufacturing. It shall be considered discrimination for purposes of section 202 of this Act and section 504 of the Rehabilitation Act of 1973 (29 U.S.C. 794) for a person to remanufacture a rail passenger car for use in intercity or commuter rail transportation so as to extend its usable life for 10 years or more, unless the rail car, to the maximum extent feasible, is made readily accessible to and usable by individuals with disabilities, including individuals who use wheelchairs, as prescribed by the Secretary of Transportation in regulations issued under section 244.

(2) Purchase or lease. It shall be considered discrimination for purposes of section 202 of this Act and section 504 of the Rehabilitation

Act of 1973 (29 U.S.C. 794) for a person to purchase or lease a remanufactured rail passenger car for use in intercity or commuter rail transportation unless such car was remanufactured in accordance with paragraph (1).

(e) Stations

(1) New stations. It shall be considered discrimination for purposes of section 202 of this Act and section 504 of the Rehabilitation Act of 1973 (29 U.S.C. 794) for a person to build a new station for use in intercity or commuter rail transportation that is not readily accessible to and usable by individuals with disabilities, including individuals who use wheelchairs, as prescribed by the Secretary of Transportation in regulations issued under section 244.

(2) Existing stations.

(A) Failure to make readily accessible.

(i) General rule. It shall be considered discrimination for purposes of section 202 of this Act and section 504 of the Rehabilitation Act of 1973 (29 U.S.C. 794) for a responsible person to fail to make existing stations in the intercity rail transportation system, and existing key stations in commuter rail transportation systems, readily accessible to and usable by individuals with disabilities, including individuals who use wheelchairs, as prescribed by the Secretary of Transportation in regulations issued under section 244.

(ii) Period for compliance (Omitted)

(iii) Designation of key stations (Omitted)

(iv) Plans and milestones (Omitted)

(B) Requirement when making alterations.

(i) General rule. It shall be considered discrimination, for purposes of section 202 of this Act and section 504 of the Rehabilitation Act of 1973 (29 U.S.C. 794), with respect to alterations of an existing station or part thereof in the intercity or commuter rail transportation systems that affect or could affect the usability of the station or part thereof, for the responsible person, owner, or person in control of the station to fail to make the alterations in such a manner that, to the maximum extent feasible, the altered portions of the station are readily accessible to and usable by individuals with disabilities, including individuals who use wheelchairs, upon completion of such alterations.

(ii) Alterations to a primary function area. It shall be considered discrimination, for purposes of section 202 of this Act and section 504 of the Rehabilitation Act of 1973 (29 U.S.C. 794), with respect to alterations that affect or could affect the usability of or access to an area of the station containing a primary function, for the responsible person, owner, or person in control of the station to fail to make the alterations in such a manner that, to the maximum extent feasible, the path of travel to the altered area, and the bathrooms, telephones, and drinking fountains serving the altered area, are readily accessible to and usable by individuals with disabilities, including individuals who use wheelchairs, upon completion of such alterations, where such alterations to the path of travel or the bathrooms, telephones, and drinking fountains serving the altered area are not disproportionate to the overall alterations in terms of cost and scope (as determined under criteria established by the Attorney General).

(C) Required cooperation. It shall be considered discrimination for purposes of section 202 of this Act and section 504 of the Rehabilitation Act of 1973 (29 U.S.C. 794) for an owner, or person in control, of a station governed by subparagraph (A) or (B) to fail to provide reasonable cooperation to a responsible person with respect to such station in that responsible persons efforts to comply with such subparagraph. An owner, or person in control, of a station shall be liable to a responsible person for any failure to provide reasonable cooperation as required by this subparagraph. Failure to receive reasonable cooperation required by this subparagraph shall not be a defense to a claim of discrimination under this Act.

SEC. 12163. CONFORMANCE OF ACCESSIBILITY STANDARDS [SECTION 243]

Accessibility standards included in regulations issued under this part shall be consistent with the minimum guidelines issued by the Architectural and Transportation Barriers Compliance Board under section 504(a) of this Act.

SEC. 12164. REGULATIONS [SECTION 244]

Not later than 1 year after the date of enactment of this Act, the Secretary of Transportation shall issue regulations, in an accessible format, necessary for carrying out this part.

SEC. 12165. INTERIM ACCESSIBILITY REQUIREMENTS [SECTION 245] (OMITTED)

SUBCHAPTER III - PUBLIC ACCOMMODATIONS AND SERVICES OPERATED BY PRIVATE ENTITIES [TITLE III]

SEC. 12181. DEFINITIONS [SECTION 301]

As used in this title:

(1) Commerce. The term commerce means travel, trade, traffic, commerce, transportation, or communication (A) among the several States; (B) between any foreign country or any territory or possession and any State; or (C) between points in the same State but through another State or foreign country.

(2) Commercial facilities. The term commercial facilities means facilities (A) that are intended for nonresidential use; and (B) whose operations will affect commerce. Such term shall not include railroad locomotives, railroad freight cars, railroad cabooses, railroad cars described in section 242 or covered under this title, railroad rights-of-way, or facilities that are covered or expressly exempted from coverage under the Fair Housing Act of 1968 (42 U.S.C. 3601 et seq.).

(3) Demand responsive system. The term demand responsive system means any system of providing transportation of individuals by a vehicle, other than a system which is a fixed route system.

(4) Fixed route system. The term fixed route system means a system of providing transportation of individuals (other than by aircraft) on which a vehicle is operated along a prescribed route according to a fixed schedule.

(5) Over-the-road bus. The term over-the-road bus means a bus characterized by an elevated passenger deck located over a baggage compartment.

(6) Private entity. The term private entity means any entity other than a public entity (as defined in section 201(1)).

(7) Public accommodation. The following private entities are considered public accommodations for purposes of this title, if the operations of such entities affect commerce (A) an inn, hotel, motel, or other place of lodging, except for an establishment located within a building that contains not more than five rooms for rent or hire and that is actually occupied by the proprietor of such establishment as the residence of such proprietor; (B) a restaurant, bar, or other establishment serving food or drink; (C) a motion picture house, theater, concert hall, stadium, or other place of exhibition or entertainment; (D)

an auditorium, convention center, lecture hall, or other place of public gathering; (E) a bakery, grocery store, clothing store, hardware store, shopping center, or other sales or rental establishment; (F) a laundromat, dry-cleaner, bank, barber shop, beauty shop, travel service, shoe repair service, funeral parlor, gas station, office of an accountant or lawyer, pharmacy, insurance office, professional office of a health care provider, hospital, or other service establishment; (G) a terminal, depot, or other station used for specified public transportation; (H) a museum, library, gallery, or other place of public display or collection; (I) a park, zoo, amusement park, or other place of recreation; (J) a nursery, elementary, secondary, undergraduate, or postgraduate private school, or other place of education; (K) a day care center, senior citizen center, homeless shelter, food bank, adoption agency, or other social service center establishment; and (L) a gymnasium, health spa, bowling alley, golf course, or other place of exercise or recreation.

(8) Rail and railroad. The terms rail and railroad have the meaning given the term railroad in section 202(e) of the Federal Railroad Safety Act of 1970 (45 U.S.C. 431(e)).

(9) Readily achievable. The term readily achievable means easily accomplishable and able to be carried out without much difficulty or expense. In determining whether an action is readily achievable, factors to be considered include (A) the nature and cost of the action needed under this Act; (B) the overall financial resources of the facility or facilities involved in the action; the number of persons employed at such facility; the effect on expenses and resources, or the impact otherwise of such action upon the operation of the facility; (C) the overall financial resources of the covered entity; the overall size of the business of a covered entity with respect to the number of its employees; the number, type, and location of its facilities; and (D) the type of operation or operations of the covered entity, including the composition, structure, and functions of the workforce of such entity; the geographic separateness, administrative or fiscal relationship of the facility or facilities in question to the covered entity.

(10) Specified public transportation. The term specified public transportation means transportation by bus, rail, or any other conveyance (other than by aircraft) that provides the general public with general or special service (including charter service) on a regular and continuing basis.

(11) Vehicle. The term vehicle does not include a rail passenger car, railroad locomotive, railroad freight car, railroad caboose, or a railroad car described in section 242 or covered under this title.

SEC. 12182. PROHIBITION OF DISCRIMINATION BY PUBLIC ACCOMMODATIONS [SECTION 302]

(a) General Rule. No individual shall be discriminated against on the basis of disability in the full and equal enjoyment of the goods, services, facilities, privileges, advantages, or accommodations of any place of public accommodation by any person who owns, leases (or leases to), or operates a place of public accommodation.

(b) Construction.

(1) General prohibition.

(A) Activities.

(i) Denial of participation. It shall be discriminatory to subject an individual or class of individuals on the basis of a disability or disabilities of such individual or class, directly, or through contractual, licensing, or other arrangements, to a denial of the opportunity of the individual or class to participate in or benefit from the goods, services, facilities, privileges, advantages, or accommodations of an entity.

(ii) Participation in unequal benefit. It shall be discriminatory to afford an individual or class of individuals, on the basis of a disability or disabilities of such individual or class, directly, or through contractual, licensing, or other arrangements with the opportunity to participate in or benefit from a good, service, facility, privilege, advantage, or accommodation that is not equal to that afforded to other individuals.

(iii) Separate benefit. It shall be discriminatory to provide an individual or class of individuals, on the basis of a disability or disabilities of such individual or class, directly, or through contractual, licensing, or other arrangements with a good, service, facility, privilege, advantage, or accommodation that is different or separate from that provided to other individuals, unless such action is necessary to provide the individual or class of individuals with a good, service, facility, privilege, advantage, or accommodation, or other opportunity that is as effective as that provided to others.

(iv) Individual or class of individuals. For purposes of clauses (i) through (iii) of this subparagraph, the term individual or class of individuals refers to the clients or customers of the covered public accommodation that enters into the contractual, licensing or other arrangement.

(B) Integrated settings. Goods, services, facilities, privileges, advantages, and accommodations shall be afforded to an individual with a disability in the most integrated setting appropriate to the needs of the individual.

(C) Opportunity to participate. Notwithstanding the existence of separate or different programs or activities provided in accordance with this section, an individual with a disability shall not be denied the opportunity to participate in such programs or activities that are not separate or different.

(D) Administrative methods. An individual or entity shall not, directly or through contractual or other arrangements, utilize standards or criteria or methods of administration (i) that have the effect of discriminating on the basis of disability; or (ii) that perpetuate the discrimination of others who are subject to common administrative control.

(E) Association. It shall be discriminatory to exclude or otherwise deny equal goods, services, facilities, privileges, advantages, accommodations, or other opportunities to an individual or entity because of the known disability of an individual with whom the individual or entity is known to have a relationship or association.

(2) Specific prohibitions (Omitted)

(3) Specific Construction. Nothing in this title shall require an entity to permit an individual to participate in or benefit from the goods, services, facilities, privileges, advantages and accommodations of such entity where such individual poses a direct threat to the health or safety of others. The term direct threat means a significant risk to the health or safety of others that cannot be eliminated by a modification of policies, practices, or procedures or by the provision of auxiliary aids or services.

SEC. 12183. NEW CONSTRUCTION AND ALTERATIONS IN PUBLIC ACCOMMODATIONS AND COMMERCIAL FACILITIES [SECTION 302] (OMITTED)

SEC. 12184. PROHIBITION OF DISCRIMINATION IN SPECIFIED PUBLIC TRANSPORTATION SERVICES PROVIDED BY PRIVATE ENTITIES [SECTION 303]

(a) General Rule. No individual shall be discriminated against on the basis of disability in the full and equal enjoyment of specified public transportation services provided by a private entity that is primarily engaged in the business of transporting people and whose operations affect commerce.

(b) Construction

For purposes of subsection (a) of this section, discrimination includes

(1) the imposition or application by an entity described in subsection (a) of eligibility criteria that screen out or tend to screen out an individual with a disability or any class of individuals with disabilities from fully enjoying the specified public transportation services provided by the entity, unless such criteria can be shown to be necessary for the provision of the services being offered;

(2) the failure of such entity to

(A) make reasonable modifications consistent with those required under section 12182(a)(2)(a)(ii) of this title;

(B) provide auxiliary aids and services consistent with the requirements of section 12182(a)(2)(a)(iii) of this title; and

(C) remove barriers consistent with the requirements of section 12182(b)(2)(A) of this title and with the requirements of section 12183(a)(2) of this title;

(3) the purchase or lease by such entity of a new vehicle (other than an automobile, a van with a seating capacity of less than 8 passengers, including the driver, or an over- the-road bus) which is to be used to provide specified public transportation and for which a solicitation is made after the 30th day following the effective date of this section, that is not readily accessible to and usable by individuals with disabilities, including individuals who use wheelchairs; except that the new vehicle need not be readily accessible to and usable by such individuals if the new vehicle is to be used solely in a demand responsive system and if the entity can demonstrate that such system, when viewed in its entirety, provides a level of service to such individuals equivalent to the level of service provided to the general public;

(4) (A) the purchase or lease by such entity of an over-the-road bus which does not comply with the regulations issued under section 12186(a)(2) of this title; and

(B) any other failure of such entity to comply with such regulations; and

(5) the purchase or lease by such entity of a new van with a seating capacity of less than 8 passengers, including the driver, which is to

be used to provide specified public transportation and for which a solicitation is made after the 30th day following the effective date of this section that is not readily accessible to or usable by individuals with disabilities, including individuals who use wheelchairs; except that the new van need not be readily accessible to and usable by such individuals if the entity can demonstrate that the system for which the van is being purchased or leased, when viewed in its entirety, provides a level of service to such individuals equivalent to the level of service provided to the general public;

(6) the purchase or lease by such entity of a new rail passenger car that is to be used to provide specified public transportation, and for which a solicitation is made later than 30 days after the effective date of this paragraph, that is not readily accessible to and usable by individuals with disabilities, including individuals who use wheelchairs; and

(7) the remanufacture by such entity of a rail passenger car that is to be used to provide specified public transportation so as to extend its usable life for 10 years or more, or the purchase or lease by such entity of such a rail car, unless the rail car, to the maximum extent feasible, is made readily accessible to and usable by individuals with disabilities, including individuals who use wheelchairs.

(c) Historical or antiquated cars

(1) Exception

To the extent that compliance with subsection (a)(2)(C) or (a)(7) of this section would significantly alter the historic or antiquated character of a historical or antiquated rail passenger car, or a rail station served exclusively by such cars, or would result in violation of any rule, regulation, standard, or order issued by the Secretary of Transportation under the Federal Railroad Safety Act of 1970, such compliance shall not be required.

(2) Definition

As used in this subsection, the term "historical or antiquated rail passenger car" means a rail passenger car

(A) which is not less than 30 years old at the time of its use for transporting individuals;

(B) the manufacturer of which is no longer in the business of manufacturing rail passenger cars; and

(C) which

(i) has a consequential association with events or persons significant to the past; or

(ii) embodies, or is being restored to embody, the distinctive characteristics of a type of rail passenger car used in the past, or to represent a time period which has passed.

SEC. 12185. STUDY [SECTION 304] (OMITTED)

SEC. 12186. REGULATIONS [SECTION 305] (OMITTED)

SEC. 12187. EXEMPTIONS FOR PRIVATE CLUBS AND RELIGIOUS ORGANIZATIONS [SECTION 306]

The provisions of this title shall not apply to private clubs or establishments exempted from coverage under title II of the Civil Rights Act of 1964 (42 U.S.C. 2000-a(e)) or to religious organizations or entities controlled by religious organizations, including places of worship.

SEC. 12188. ENFORCEMENT [SECTION 307]

(a) In General.

(1) Availability of remedies and procedures. The remedies and procedures set forth in section 204(a) of the Civil Rights Act of 1964 (42 U. S. C. 2000a-3(a)) are the remedies and procedures this title provides to any person who is being subjected to discrimination on the basis of disability in violation of this title or who has reasonable grounds for believing that such person is about to be subjected to discrimination in violation of section 303. Nothing in this section shall require a person with a disability to engage in a futile gesture if such person has actual notice that a person or organization covered by this title does not intend to comply with its provisions.

(2) Injunctive relief. In the case of violations of sections 302(b)(2)(A)(iv) and section 303(a), injunctive relief shall include an order to alter facilities to make such facilities readily accessible to and usable by individuals with disabilities to the extent required by this title. Where appropriate, injunctive relief shall also include requiring the provision of an auxiliary aid or service, modification of a policy, or provision of alternative methods, to the extent required by this title.

(b) Enforcement by the Attorney General.

(1) Denial of rights.

(A) Duty to investigate.

(i) In general. The Attorney General shall investigate alleged violations of this title, and shall undertake periodic reviews of compliance of covered entities under this title.

(ii) Attorney General Certification. On the application of a State or local government, the Attorney General may, in consultation with the Architectural and Transportation Barriers Compliance Board, and after prior notice and a public hearing at which persons, including individuals with disabilities, are provided an opportunity to testify against such certification, certify that a State law or local building code or similar ordinance that establishes accessibility requirements meets or exceeds the minimum requirements of this Act for the accessibility and usability of covered facilities under this title. At any enforcement proceeding under this section, such certification by the Attorney General shall be rebuttable evidence that such State law or local ordinance does meet or exceed the minimum requirements of this Act.

(B) Potential violation. If the Attorney General has reasonable cause to believe that (i) any person or group of persons is engaged in a pattern or practice of discrimination under this title; or (ii) any person or group of persons has been discriminated against under this title and such discrimination raises an issue of general public importance, the Attorney General may commence a civil action in any appropriate United States district court.

(2) Authority of court. In a civil action under paragraph (1)(B), the court (A) may grant any equitable relief that such court considers to be appropriate, including, to the extent required by this title (i) granting temporary, preliminary, or permanent relief; (ii) providing an auxiliary aid or service, modification of policy, practice, or procedure, or alternative method; and (iii) making facilities readily accessible to and usable by individuals with disabilities; (B) may award such other relief as the court considers to be appropriate, including monetary damages to persons aggrieved when requested by the Attorney General; and (C) may, to vindicate the public interest, assess a civil penalty against the entity in an amount (i) not exceeding $50,000 for a first violation; and (ii) not exceeding $100,000 for any subsequent violation.

(3) Single violation. For purposes of paragraph (2)(C), in determining whether a first or subsequent violation has occurred, a determination in a single action, by judgment or settlement, that

the covered entity has engaged in more than one discriminatory act shall be counted as a single violation.

(4) Punitive damages. For purposes of subsection (b)(2)(B), the term monetary damages and such other relief does not include punitive damages.

(5) Judicial consideration. In a civil action under paragraph (1)(B), the court, when considering what amount of civil penalty, if any, is appropriate, shall give consideration to any good faith effort or attempt to comply with this Act by the entity. In evaluating good faith, the court shall consider, among other factors it deems relevant, whether the entity could have reasonably anticipated the need for an appropriate type of auxiliary aid needed to accommodate the unique needs of a particular individual with a disability.

SEC. 12189. EXAMINATIONS AND COURSES [SECTION 308]

Any person that offers examinations or courses related to applications, licensing, certification, or credentialing for secondary or post-secondary education, professional, or trade purposes shall offer such examinations or courses in a place and manner accessible to persons with disabilities or offer alternative accessible arrangements for such individuals.

SUBCHAPTER IV. MISCELLANEOUS PROVISIONS [TITLE V]

SEC. 12201. CONSTRUCTION [SECTION 501]

(a) In General. Except as otherwise provided in this Act, nothing in this Act shall be construed to apply a lesser standard than the standards applied under title V of the Rehabilitation Act of 1973 (29 U.S.C. 790 et seq.) or the regulations issued by Federal agencies pursuant to such title.

(b) Relationship to Other Laws. Nothing in this Act shall be construed to invalidate or limit the remedies, rights, and procedures of any Federal law or law of any State or political subdivision of any State or jurisdiction that provides greater or equal protection for the rights of individuals with disabilities than are afforded by this Act. Nothing in this Act shall be construed to preclude the prohibition of, or the imposition of restrictions on, smoking in places of employment covered by title I, in transportation covered by title II or III, or in places of public accommodation covered by title III.

(c) Insurance. Titles I through IV of this Act shall not be construed to prohibit or restrict (1) an insurer, hospital or medical service company, health maintenance organization, or any agent, or entity that administers benefit plans, or similar organizations from underwriting risks, classifying risks, or administering such risks that are based on or not inconsistent with State law; or (2) a person or organization covered by this Act from establishing, sponsoring, observing or administering the terms of a bona fide benefit plan that are based on underwriting risks, classifying risks, or administering such risks that are based on or not inconsistent with State law; or (3) a person or organization covered by this Act from establishing, sponsoring, observing or administering the terms of a bona fide benefit plan that is not subject to State laws that regulate insurance. Paragraphs (1), (2), and (3) shall not be used as a subterfuge to evade the purposes of title I and III.

(d) Accommodations and Services. Nothing in this Act shall be construed to require an individual with a disability to accept an accommodation, aid, service, opportunity, or benefit which such individual chooses not to accept.

SEC. 12202. STATE IMMUNITY [SECTION 502]

A State shall not be immune under the eleventh amendment to the Constitution of the United States from an action in Federal or State court of competent jurisdiction for a violation of this Act. In any action against a State for a violation of the requirements of this Act, remedies (including remedies both at law and in equity) are available for such a violation to the same extent as such remedies are available for such a violation in an action against any public or private entity other than a State.

SEC. 12203. PROHIBITION AGAINST RETALIATION AND COERCION [SECTION 503]

(a) Retaliation. No person shall discriminate against any individual because such individual has opposed any act or practice made unlawful by this Act or because such individual made a charge, testified, assisted, or participated in any manner in an investigation, proceeding, or hearing under this Act.

(b) Interference, Coercion, or Intimidation. It shall be unlawful to coerce, intimidate, threaten, or interfere with any individual in the exercise or enjoyment of, or on account of his or her having exercised or enjoyed, or on account of his or her having aided or encouraged any other individual in the exercise or enjoyment of, any right granted or protected by this Act.

(c) Remedies and Procedures. The remedies and procedures available under sections 107, 203, and 308 of this Act shall be available to aggrieved persons for violations of subsections (a) and (b), with respect to title I, title II and title III, respectively.

SEC. 12204. REGULATIONS BY THE ARCHITECTURAL AND TRANSPORTATION BARRIERS COMPLIANCE BOARD [SECTION 504] (OMITTED)

SEC. 12205. ATTORNEYS FEES [SECTION 505]

In any action or administrative proceeding commenced pursuant to this Act, the court or agency, in its discretion, may allow the prevailing party, other than the United States, a reasonable attorneys fee, including litigation expenses, and costs, and the United States shall be liable for the foregoing the same as a private individual.

SEC. 12206. TECHNICAL ASSISTANCE [SECTION 506]

(a) Plan for Assistance (Omitted)

(b) Agency and Public Assistance (Omitted)

(c) Implementation.

(1) Rendering assistance (Omitted)

(2) Implementation of titles.

(A) Title I. The Equal Employment Opportunity Commission and the Attorney General shall implement the plan for assistance developed under subsection (a), for title I.

(B) Title II.

(i) Subtitle a. The Attorney General shall implement such plan for assistance for subtitle A of title II.

(ii) Subtitle b. The Secretary of Transportation shall implement such plan for assistance for subtitle B of title II.

(C) Title III. The Attorney General, in coordination with the Secretary of Transportation and the Chair of the Architectural Transportation Barriers Compliance Board, shall implement such plan for assistance for title III, except for section 304, the plan for assistance for which shall be implemented by the Secretary of Transportation.

(D) Title IV. The Chairman of the Federal Communications Commission, in coordination with the Attorney General, shall implement such plan for assistance for title IV.

(3) Technical assistance manuals (Omitted)

(d) Grants and Contracts (Omitted)

(e) Failure to Receive Assistance (Omitted)

SEC. 12207. FEDERAL WILDERNESS AREAS [SECTION 507] (OMITTED)

SEC. 12208. TRANSVESTITES [SECTION 508]

For the purposes of this Act, the term disabled or disability shall not apply to an individual solely because that individual is a transvestite.

SEC. 12209. INSTRUMENTALITIES OF CONGRESS [SECTION 509] (OMITTED)

SEC. 12210. ILLEGAL USE OF DRUGS [SECTION 510]

(a) In General. For purposes of this Act, the term individual with a disability does not include an individual who is currently engaging in the illegal use of drugs, when the covered entity acts on the basis of such use.

(b) Rules of Construction. Nothing in subsection (a) shall be construed to exclude as an individual with a disability an individual who (1) has successfully completed a supervised drug rehabilitation program and is no longer engaging in the illegal use of drugs, or has otherwise been rehabilitated successfully and is no longer engaging in such use; (2) is participating in a supervised rehabilitation program and is no longer engaging in such use; or (3) is erroneously regarded as engaging in such use, but is not engaging in such use; except that it shall not be a violation of this Act for a covered entity to adopt or administer reasonable policies or procedures, including but not limited to drug testing, designed to ensure that an individual described in paragraph (1) or (2) is no longer engaging in the illegal use of drugs; however, nothing in this section shall be construed to encourage, prohibit, restrict, or authorize the conducting of testing for the illegal use of drugs.

(c) Health and Other Services. Notwithstanding subsection (a) and section 511(b)(3), an individual shall not be denied health services, or services provided in connection with drug rehabilitation, on the basis of the current illegal use of drugs if the individual is otherwise entitled to such services.

(d) "Illegal use of drugs" defined.

(1) In general. The term illegal use of drugs means the use of drugs, the possession or distribution of which is unlawful under the Controlled Substances Act (21 U.S.C. 812). Such term does not include the use of a drug taken under supervision by a licensed

health care professional, or other uses authorized by the Controlled Substances Act or other provisions of Federal law.

(2) Drugs. The term drug means a controlled substance, as defined in schedules I through V of section 202 of the Controlled Substances Act.

SEC. 12211. DEFINITIONS. [SECTION 511]

(a) Homosexuality and Bisexuality. For purposes of the definition of disability in section 3(2), homosexuality and bisexuality are not impairments and as such are not disabilities under this Act.

(b) Certain Conditions. Under this Act, the term disability shall not include (1) transvestism, transsexualism, pedophilia, exhibitionism, voyeurism, gender identity disorders not resulting from physical impairments, or other sexual behavior disorders; (2) compulsive gambling, kleptomania, or pyromania; or (3) psychoactive substance use disorders resulting from current illegal use of drugs.

SEC. 12212. ALTERNATIVE MEANS OF DISPUTE RESOLUTION [SECTION 513]

Where appropriate and to the extent authorized by law, the use of alternative means of dispute resolution, including settlement negotiations, conciliation, facilitation, mediation, factfinding, minitrials, and arbitration, is encouraged to resolve disputes arising under this Act.

SSEC. 12213. SEVERABILITY [SECTION 514]

Should any provision in this Act be found to be unconstitutional by a court of law, such provision shall be severed from the remainder of the Act, and such action shall not affect the enforceability of the remaining provisions of the Act.

* * *

TITLE 47 - TELEGRAPHS, TELEPHONES, AND RADIOTELEGRAPHS

CHAPTER 5 - WIRE OR RADIO COMMUNICATION

SUBCHAPTER II - COMMON CARRIERS

PART I - COMMON CARRIER REGULATION

SEC. 225. TELECOMMUNICATIONS SERVICES FOR HEARING-IMPAIRED AND SPEECH-IMPAIRED INDIVIDUALS [SECTION 401]

(a) Definitions

As used in this section

(1) Common carrier or carrier

The term "common carrier" or "carrier" includes any common carrier engaged in interstate communication by wire or radio as defined in section 153 of this title and any common carrier engaged in intrastate communication by wire or radio, notwithstanding sections 152(a) and 221(a) of this title.

(2) TDD

The term "TDD" means a Telecommunications Device for the Deaf which is a machine that employs graphic communication in the transmission of coded signals through a wire or radio communication system.

(3) Telecommunications relay services

The term "telecommunications relay services" means telephone transmission services that provide the ability for an individual who has a hearing impairment or speech impairment to engage in communication by wire or radio with a hearing individual in a manner that is functionally equivalent to the ability of an individual who does not have a hearing impairment or speech impairment to communicate using voice communication services by wire or radio. Such term includes services that enable two-way communication between an individual who uses a TDD or other nonvoice terminal device and an individual who does not use such a device.

(b) Availability of telecommunications relay service

(1) In general

In order to carry out the purposes established under section 151 of this title, to make available to all individuals in the United States a rapid, efficient nationwide communication service, and to increase the utility of the telephone system of the Nation, the Commission shall ensure that interstate and intrastate telecommunications relay services are available, to the extent possible and in the most efficient manner, to hearing-impaired and speech-impaired individuals in the United States.

(2) Use of general authority and remedies

For the purposes of administering and enforcing the provisions of this section and the regulations prescribed thereunder, the Commission shall have the same authority, power, and functions with respect to common carriers engaged in intrastate communication as the Commission has in administering and enforcing the provisions of this subchapter with respect to any common carrier engaged in interstate communication. Any violation of this section by any common carrier engaged in intrastate communication shall be subject to the same remedies, penalties, and procedures as are applicable to a violation of this chapter by a common carrier engaged in interstate communication.

(c) Provision of services

Each common carrier providing telephone voice transmission services shall, not later than 3 years after July 26, 1990, provide in compliance with the regulations prescribed under this section, throughout the area in which it offers service, telecommunications relay services, individually, through designees, through a competitively selected vendor, or in concert with other carriers. A common carrier shall be considered to be in compliance with such regulations

(1) with respect to intrastate telecommunications relay services in any State that does not have a certified program under subsection (f) of this section and with respect to interstate telecommunications relay services, if such common carrier (or other entity through which the carrier is providing such relay services) is in compliance with the Commission's regulations under subsection (d) of this section; or

(2) with respect to intrastate telecommunications relay services in any State that has a certified program under subsection (f) of this section for such State, if such common carrier (or other entity through which the carrier is providing such relay services) is in compliance with the program certified under subsection (f) of this section for such State.

(d) Regulations

(1) In general

The Commission shall, not later than 1 year after July 26, 1990, prescribe regulations to implement this section, including regulations that

(A) establish functional requirements, guidelines, and operations procedures for telecommunications relay services;

(B) establish minimum standards that shall be met in carrying out subsection (c) of this section;

(C) require that telecommunications relay services operate every day for 24 hours per day;

(D) require that users of telecommunications relay services pay rates no greater than the rates paid for functionally equivalent voice communication services with respect to such factors as the duration of the call, the time of day, and the distance from point of origination to point of termination;

(E) prohibit relay operators from failing to fulfill the obligations of common carriers by refusing calls or limiting the length of calls that use telecommunications relay services;

(F) prohibit relay operators from disclosing the content of any relayed conversation and from keeping records of the content of any such conversation beyond the duration of the call; and

(G) prohibit relay operators from intentionally altering a relayed conversation.

(2) Technology

The Commission shall ensure that regulations prescribed to implement this section encourage, consistent with section 157(a) of this title, the use of existing technology and do not discourage or impair the development of improved technology.

(3) Jurisdictional separation of costs

(A) In general

Consistent with the provisions of section 410 of this title, the Commission shall prescribe regulations governing the jurisdictional separation of costs for the services provided pursuant to this section.

(B) Recovering costs

Such regulations shall generally provide that costs caused by interstate telecommunications relay services shall be recovered from all subscribers for every interstate service and costs caused by intrastate telecommunications relay services shall be recovered from the intrastate jurisdiction. In a State that has a certified program under subsection (f) of this section, a State commission shall permit a common carrier to recover the costs incurred in providing intrastate telecommunications relay services by a method consistent with the requirements of this section.

(e) Enforcement

(1) In general

Subject to subsections (f) and (g) of this section, the Commission shall enforce this section.

(2) Complaint

The Commission shall resolve, by final order, a complaint alleging a violation of this section within 180 days after the date such complaint is filed.

(f) Certification

(1) State documentation

Any State desiring to establish a State program under this section shall submit documentation to the Commission that describes the program of such State for implementing intrastate telecommunications relay services and the procedures and remedies available for enforcing any requirements imposed by the State program.

(2) Requirements for certification

After review of such documentation, the Commission shall certify the State program if the Commission determines that

(A) the program makes available to hearing-impaired and speech-impaired individuals, either directly, through designees, through a competitively selected vendor, or through regulation of intrastate common carriers, intrastate telecommunications relay services in such State in a manner that meets or exceeds the requirements of regulations prescribed by the Commission under subsection (d) of this section; and

(B) the program makes available adequate procedures and remedies for enforcing the requirements of the State program.

(3) Method of funding

Except as provided in subsection (d) of this section, the Commission shall not refuse to certify a State program based solely on the method such State will implement for funding intrastate telecommunication relay services.

(4) Suspension or revocation of certification

The Commission may suspend or revoke such certification if, after notice and opportunity for hearing, the Commission determines that such certification is no longer warranted. In a State whose program has been suspended or revoked, the Commission shall take such steps as may be necessary, consistent with this section, to ensure continuity of telecommunications relay services.

(g) Complaint

(1) Referral of complaint

If a complaint to the Commission alleges a violation of this section with respect to intrastate telecommunications relay services within a State and certification of the program of such State under subsection (f) of this section is in effect, the Commission shall refer such complaint to such State.

(2) Jurisdiction of Commission

After referring a complaint to a State under paragraph (1), the Commission shall exercise jurisdiction over such complaint only if

(A) final action under such State program has not been taken on such complaint by such State

(i) within 180 days after the complaint is filed with such State; or

(ii) within a shorter period as prescribed by the regulations of such State; or

(B) the Commission determines that such State program is no longer qualified for certification under subsection (f) of this section.

SUBCHAPTER VI - MISCELLANEOUS PROVISIONS

SEC. 611. CLOSED-CAPTIONING OF PUBLIC SERVICE ANNOUNCEMENTS [SECTION 402]

Any television public service announcement that is produced or funded in whole or in part by any agency or instrumentality of Federal Government shall include closed captioning of the verbal content of such announcement. A television broadcast station licensee

(1) shall not be required to supply closed captioning for any such announcement that fails to include it; and

(2) shall not be liable for broadcasting any such announcement without transmitting a closed caption unless the licensee intentionally fails to transmit the closed caption that was included with the announcement.

APPENDIX 5:

RESOURCE DIRECTORY - NATIONAL DISABILITY ORGANIZATIONS

ORGANIZATION	ADDRESS	TELEPHONE	E-MAIL	WEBSITE
Alexander Graham Bell Association for the Deaf and Hard of Hearing	3417 Volta Place NW Washington, DC 20007	202-337-5220	parents@agbell.org	www.agbell.org
Alliance for Technology Access	1304 Southpoint Blvd. Suite 240 Petaluma, CA 94954	707-778-3011	atainfo@ataccess.org	www.ataccess.org
American Association of Kidney Patients (AAKP)	3505 Frontage Road Suite 315 Tampa, FL 33607	800-749-2257	info@aakp.org	www.aakp.org
American Association of Suicidology	5221 Wisconsin Ave, NW Washington, DC 20015	202-237-2280	info@suicidology.org	www.suicidology.org

ORGANIZATION	ADDRESS	TELEPHONE	E-MAIL	WEBSITE
American Brain Tumor Association	2720 River Road Des Moines, IA 60018	847-827-9910	info@abta.org	www.abta.org
American Council of the Blind	1155 15th Street NW Suite 1004 Washington, DC 20005	202-467-5081	info@acb.org	www.acb.org
American Diabetes Association	1701 N. Beauregard St. Alexandria, VA 22311	703-549-1500	AskADA@diabetes.org	www.diabetes.org
American Foundation for the Blind (AFB)	11 Penn Plaza Suite 300 New York, NY 10001	212-502-7662	abinfo@afb.net	www.afb.org
American Heart Association	7272 Greenville Ave. Dallas, TX 75231	214-373-6300	inquire@amhrt.org	www.americanheart.org
American Liver Foundation	75 Maiden Lane Suite 603 New York, NY 10038	212-668-1000	info@liverfoundation.org	www.liverfoundation.org
American Lung Association	61 Broadway, 6th Floor New York, NY 10006	212-315-8700	e-mail via website	www.lungusa.org
American Occupational Therapy Association	4720 Montgomery Lane P.O. Box 31220 Bethesda, MD 20824	301-652-2682	none listed	www.aota.org

ORGANIZATION	ADDRESS	TELEPHONE	E-MAIL	WEBSITE
American Physical Therapy Association	1111 North Fairfax St. Alexandria, VA 22314	703-684-2782	practice@apta.org	www.apta.org
American Society for Deaf Children	P.O. Box 3355 Gettysburg, PA 17325	800-942-2732	asdc@deafchildren.org	www.deafchildren.org
American Speech-Language-Hearing Association (ASHA)	10801 Rockville Pike Rockville, MD 20852	301-897-5700	actioncenter@asha.org	www.asha.org
American Syringomyelia Alliance Project	P.O. Box 1586 Longview, TX 75606	903-236-7079	info@asap.org	www.asap.org
American Therapeutic Recreation Assoc.	1414 Prince Street Suite 204 Alexandria, VA 22314	703-683-9420	atra@atra-tr.org	www.atra-tr.org
Angelman Syndrome Foundation	3015 E. New York St. Suite A2265 Aurora, IL 60504	630-978-4245	info@angelman.org	www.angelman.org
Anxiety Disorders Association of America	8730 Georgia Avenue Suite 600 Silver Spring, MD 20910	240-485-1001	AnxDis@adaa.org	www.adaa.org
Aplastic Anemia & MDS International Foundation, Inc.	P.O. Box 613 Annapolis, MD 21404	410-867-0242	help@aamds.org	www.aamds.org

ORGANIZATION	ADDRESS	TELEPHONE	E-MAIL	WEBSITE
The ARC	1010 Wayne Avenue Suite 650 Silver Spring, MD 20910	301-565-3842	info@thearc.org	www.thearc.org
ARCH National Respite Network & Resource Center	800 Eastowne Drive Suite 105 Chapel Hill, NC 27514	919-490-5577	None listed	www.archrespite.org
Arthritis Foundation	P.O. Box 7669 Atlanta, GA 30357	404-872-7100	help@arthritis.org	www.arthritis.org
Asthma and Allergy Foundation of America	1233 20th Street NW Suite 402 Washington, DC 20036	202-466-7643	info@aafa.org	www.aafa.org
Autism Society of America	7910 Woodmont Ave. Suite 300 Bethesda, MD 20814	301-657-0881	info@autism-society.org	www.autism-society.org
Beach Center on Disability	1200 Sunnyside Ave. Lawrence, KS 66045	785-864-7600	beachcenter@ku.edu	www.beachcenter.org
Best Buddies International, Inc.	100 S.E. Second Street Suite 1990 Miami, FL 33131	305-374-2233	info@bestbuddies.org	www.bestbuddies.org

ORGANIZATION	ADDRESS	TELEPHONE	E-MAIL	WEBSITE
Blind Childrens Center	4120 Marathon Street Los Angeles, CA 90029	323-664-2153	info@ blindchildrenscenter.org	www.blindchildrens center.org
Brain Injury Association of America	8201 Greensboro Drive Suite 611 McLean, VA 22102	703-761-0750	FamilyHelpline@ biausa.org	www.biausa.org
CADRE (Consortium for Appropriate Dispute Resolution in Special Education	P.O. Box 51360 Eugene, OR 97405	541-686-5060	cadre@directionservice. org	www.directionservice. org/cadre
Center for Effective Collaboration and Practice (CECP)	1000 Thomas Jefferson Street NW, Suite 400 Washington, DC 20007	202-944-5300	center@air.org	cecp.air.org
Center for Evidence Based Practice: Young Children with Challenging Behavior	13301 Bruce B. Downs Boulevard Tampa, FL 33612	813-974-6111	dunlap@fmhi.usf.edu	challengingbehavior. fmhi.usf.edu
Center for Universal Design	Campus Box 8613 Raleigh, NC 27695	919-515-3082	cud@ncsu.edu	www.design.ncsu. edu/cud
Child and Adolescent Bipolar Foundation	1000 Skokie Blvd Suite 425 Wilmette, IL 60091	847-256-8525	cabf@bpkids.org	www.bpkids.org
Childhood Apraxia of Speech Association of North America (CASANA)	123 Eisele Road Cheswick, PA 15024	412-767-6589	helpdesk@apraxia-kids.org	www.apraxia-kids.org

ORGANIZATION	ADDRESS	TELEPHONE	E-MAIL	WEBSITE
Children and Adults with Attention-Deficit/Hyperactivity Disorder (CHADD)	8181 Professional Place Suite 150 Landover, MD 20785	301-306-7070	none listed	www.chadd.org
Children's Craniofacial Association	13140 Coit Road Suite 307 Dallas, TX 75240	214-570-9099	contactCCA@ccakids.com	www.ccakids.com
Children's Tumor Foundation	95 Pine Street, 16th Fl. New York, NY 10005	212-344-6633	info@ctf.org	www.ctf.org
Chronic Fatigue and Immune Dysfunction Syndrome Association (CFIDS)	P.O. Box 220398 Charlotte, NC 28222	704-365-2343	cfids@cfids.org	www.cfids.org
Closing the Gap, Inc.	P.O. Box 68 526 Main Street Henderson, MN 56044	507-248-3294	none listed	www.closingthegap.com
Council for Exceptional Children (CEC)	1110 N. Glebe Road Suite 300 Arlington, VA 22201	703-620-3660	service@cec.sped.org	www.cec.sped.org
Craniofacial Foundation of America	975 East Third Street P.O. Box 269 Chattanooga, TN 37403	423-778-9192	farmertm@erlanger.org	www.erlanger.org/craniofacial/found1.html

ORGANIZATION	ADDRESS	TELEPHONE	E-MAIL	WEBSITE
Crohn's & Colitis Foundation of America	386 Park Avenue South 17th Floor New York, NY 10016	212-685-3440	info@ccffa.org	www.ccfa.org
Cystic Fibrosis Foundation	6931 Arlington Road Bethesda, MD 20814	301-951-4422	info@cff.org	www.cff.org
Depression and Bipolar Support Alliance	730 N. Franklin Street Suite 501 Chicago, IL 60610	312-642-0049	questions@dbsalliance.org	www.dbsalliance.org
Disability Statistics Rehabilitation, Research and Training Center	3333 California Street Room 340 San Francisco, CA 94118	415-502-5210	distats@itsa.ucsf.edu	www.dsc.ucsf.edu
Disabled Sports USA	451 Hungerford Drive Suite 100 Rockville, MD 20850	301-217-0960	information@dsusa.org	www.dsusa.org
Easter Seals	230 West Monroe Street Suite 1800 Chicago, IL 60606	312-726-6200	info@easter-seals.org	www.easter-seals.org
Epilepsy Foundation	4351 Garden City Drive 5th Floor Landover, MD 20785	301-459-3700	e-mail via website	www.epilepsyfoundation.org

ORGANIZATION	ADDRESS	TELEPHONE	E-MAIL	WEBSITE
FACES: The National Craniofacial Association	P.O. Box 11082 Chattanooga, TN 37401	423-266-1632	faces@faces-cranio.org	www.faces-cranio.org
Family Center for Technology and Disabilities	1825 Connecticut Ave NW, 7th Floor Washington, DC 20009	202-884-8068	fctd@aed.org	www.fctd.info
Family Empowerment Network	772 S. Mills Street Madison, WI 53715	608-262-6590	fen@fammed.wisc.edu	www.fammed.wisc.edu/fen
Family Resource Center on Disabilities	20 East Jackson Blvd. Room 300 Chicago, IL 60604	312-939-3513	none listed	www.frcd.org
Family Village	1500 Highland Avenue Madison, WI 53705	608-265-5776	familyvillage@waisman.wisc.edu	www.familyvillage.wisc.edu
Family Voices	2340 Alamo SE Suite 102 Albuquerque, NM 87106	505-872-4774	kidshealth@familyvoices.org	www.familyvoices.org
Federation of Families for Children's Mental Health	1101 King Street Suite 420 Alexandria, VA 22314	703-684-7710	ffcmh@ffcmh.com	www.ffcmh.org
First Signs, Inc.	P.O. Box 358 Merrimac, MA 01860	978-346-4380	info@firstsigns.org	www.firstsigns.org

ORGANIZATION	ADDRESS	TELEPHONE	E-MAIL	WEBSITE
Forward Face	317 East 34th Street Suite 901A New York, NY 10016	212-684-5860	info@forwardface.org	www.forwardface.org
Foundation for Ichthyosis and Related Skin Types	1601 Valley Forge Road Lansdale, PA 19446	215-631-1411	info@scalyskin.org	www.scalyskin.org
Genetic Alliance	4301 Connecticut NW Suite 404 Washington, DC 20008	202-966-5557	info@geneticalliance. org	www.geneticalliance. org
Head Start Bureau	P.O. Box 1182 Washington, DC 20013	none listed	none listed	www.acf.dhhs.gov/ programs/hsb
Human Growth Foundation	997 Glen Cove Avenue Suite 5 Glen Head, NY 11545	800-451-6434	hgf1@hgfound.org	www.hgfound.org
Huntington's Disease Society of America	158 West 29th Street 7th Floor New York, NY 10001	212-242-1968	hdsainfo@hdsa.org	www.hdsa.org
Hydrocephalus Association	870 Market Street Suite 705 San Francisco, CA 94102	415-732-7040	info@hydroassoc.org	www.hydroassoc.org

ORGANIZATION	ADDRESS	TELEPHONE	E-MAIL	WEBSITE
IBM Accessibility Center	11400 Burnet Road Austin, TX 78758	800-426-4832	e-mail via website	www-3.ibm/com/able/ index.html
Immune Deficiency Foundation	40 W. Chesapeake Ave. Suite 308 Towson, MD 21204	800-296-4433	idf@primaryimmune. org	www.primaryimmune. org
Independent Living Research Utilization Project	2323 South Sheppard Suite 1000 Houston, TX 77019	713-520-0232	ilru@ilru.org	www.ilru.org
International Dyslexia Association	Chester Building Suite 382 8600 LaSalle Road Baltimore, MD 21286	410-296-0232	info@interdys.org	www.interdys.org
International Resource Center for Down Syndrome	1621 Euclid Avenue Suite 802 Cleveland, OH 44115	216-621-5858	none listed	none listed
International Rett Syndrome Assoc.	9121 Piscataway Road Clinton, MD 20735	301-856-3334	irsa@rettsyndrome.org	www.rettsyndrome.org
Job Accommodation Network (JAN)	P.O. Box 6080 Morgantown, WV 26506	800-526-7234	jan@jan.wvu.edu	www.jan.wvu.edu

ORGANIZATION	ADDRESS	TELEPHONE	E-MAIL	WEBSITE
Kristin Brooks Hope Center	2001 N. Beauregard St. 12th Floor Alexandria, VA 22311	703-837-3364	info@hopeline.com	www. livewithdepression.org
Learning Disabilities Association of America (LDA)	4156 Library Road Pittsburgh, PA 15234	412-341-1515	info@ldaamerica.org	www.ldaamerica.org
Let's Face It USA	P.O. Box 29972 Bellingham, WA 98228	360-676-7325	letsfaceit@faceit.org	www.faceit.org
Leukemia & Lymphoma Society	1311 Mamaroneck Ave. White Plains, NY 10605	914-949-5213	infocenter@leukemia-lymphoma.org	www.leukemia-lymphoma.org
Little People of America	5289 N.E. Elam Young Parkway, Suite F-100 Hillsboro, OR 97124	888-572-2001	info@lpaonline.org	www.lpaonline.org
Lupus Foundation of America	2000 L Street NW Suite 710 Washington, DC 20036	202-349-1155	info@lupus.org	www.lupus.org
MAAP Services for the Autism Spectrum (MAAP)	P.O. Box 524 Crown Point, IN 46308	219-662-1311	chart@netnitco.net	www.maapservices.org
MAGIC Foundation	6645 W. North Avenue Oak Park, IL 60302	708-383-0808	mary@ magicfoundation.org	www.magicfoun dation.org

ORGANIZATION	ADDRESS	TELEPHONE	E-MAIL	WEBSITE
March of Dimes Birth Defects Foundation	1275 Mamaroneck Ave. White Plains, NY 10605	914-428-7100	askus@marchofdimes. com	www.marchofdimes. com
MUMS National Parent-to-Parent Network	150 Custer Ct. Green Bay, WI 54301	920-336-5333	mums@netnet.net	www.netnet.net/mums
Muscular Dystrophy Association (MDA)	3300 East Sunrise Drive Tucson, AZ 85718	520-529-2000	mda@mdausa.org	www.mdausa.org
National Alliance for the Mentally Ill (NAMI)	Colonial Place Three 2107 Wilson Blvd. Suite 300 Arlington, VA 22201	703-524-7600	info@nami.org	www.nami.org
National Association for the Dually Diagnosed (NADD)	132 Fair Street Kingston, NY 12401	845-331-4336	info@thenadd.org	www.thenadd.org
National Association of the Deaf	814 Thayer Avenue Suite 250 Silver Spring, MD 20910	301-587-1788	nadinfo@nad.org	www.nad.org
National Association of Hospital Hospitality Houses	P.O. Box 18087 Asheville, NC 28814	828-253-1188	helpinghomes@nahhh. org	www.nahhh.org
National Association of Private Special Education Centers (NAPSEC)	1522 K Street NW Suite 1032 Washington, DC 20005	202-408-3338	napsec@aol.com	www.napsec.com

ORGANIZATION	ADDRESS	TELEPHONE	E-MAIL	WEBSITE
National Ataxia Foundation	2600 Fernbrook Lane Suite 119 Minneapolis, MN 55447	763-553-0020	naf@ataxia.org	www.ataxia.org
National Attention Deficit Disorder Association	P.O. Box 543 Pottstown, PA 19464	484-944-2101	mail@add.org	www.add.org
National Brain Tumor Foundation	22 Battery Street Suite 612 San Francisco, CA 94111	415-834-9970	nbtf@braintumor.org	www.braintumor.org
National Center for Learning Disabilities (NCLD)	381 Park Avenue South Suite 1401 New York, NY 10016	212-545-7510	help@getreadytoread. org	www.ld.org
National Center for Post-Traumatic Stress Disorder	215 North Main Street White River Junction, VT 05009	802-296-6300	ncptsd@ncptssd.org	www.ncptsd.org
National Center for Special Education Personnel and Related Service Providers	1800 Diagonal Road Suite 320 Alexandria, VA 22314	703-519-3800	e-mail via website	www.personnelcenter. org
National Center on Physical Activity and Disability (NCPAD)	1640 W. Roosevelt Road Chicago, IL 60608	800-900-8086	ncpad@uic.edu	www.ncpad.org

ORGANIZATION	ADDRESS	TELEPHONE	E-MAIL	WEBSITE
National Chronic Fatigue Syndrome and Fibromyalgia Association (NCFSFA)	P.O. Box 18426 Kansas City, MO 64133	816-313-2000	information@ncfsfa.org	www.ncfsfa.org
National Council on Independent Living	1916 Wilson Boulevard Suite 209 Arlington, VA 22201	703-525-3406	ncil@ncil.org	www.ncil.org
National Down Syndrome Congress	1370 Center Drive Suite 102 Atlanta, GA 30338	770-604-9500	info@ndsccenter.org	www.ndsccenter.org
National Down Syndrome Society	666 Broadway 8th Floor New York, NY 10012	212-460-9330	info@ndss.org	www.ndss.org
National Eating Disorders Association	603 Stewart Street Suite 803 Seattle, WA 98101	206-382-3587	info@NationalEasting Disorders.org	www.nationaleating disorders.org
National Federation for the Blind	1800 Johnson Street Baltimore, MD 21230	410-659-9314	nfb@nfb.org	www.nfb.org
National Fragile X Foundation	P.O. Box 190488 San Francisco, CA 94119	925-938-9315	NATLFX@FragileX.org	www.fragilex.org

ORGANIZATION	ADDRESS	TELEPHONE	E-MAIL	WEBSITE
National Gaucher Foundation	5410 Edson Lane Suite 260 Rockville, MD 20852	301-816-1515	ngf@gaucherdisease.org	www.gaucherdisease.org
National Kidney Foundation	30 East 33rd Street New York, NY 10016	212-889-2210	info@kidney.org	www.kidney.org
National Library Service for the Blind & Physically Handicapped	1291 Taylor Street NW Washington, DC 20011	202-707-5100	nls@loc.gov	www.loc.gov/nls
National Limb Loss Information Center	900 East Hill Avenue Suite 285 Knoxville, TN 27915	888-267-5669	nllicinfo@amputee-coalition.org	www.amputee-coalition.org/nllic_about.html
National Lymphedema Network	1611 Telegraph Avenue Suite 1111 Oakland, CA 94612	510-208-3200	nln@lymphnet.org	www.lymphnet.org
National Mental Health Association	2001 N. Beauregard 12th Floor Alexandria, VA 22311	703-684-7722	e-mail via website	www.nmha.org
National Multiple Sclerosis Society	733 Third Avenue New York, NY 10017	800-344-4867	e-mail via website	www.nationalmssociety.org

ORGANIZATION	ADDRESS	TELEPHONE	E-MAIL	WEBSITE
National Organization for Albinism and Hypopigmentation (NOAH)	P.O. Box 959 East Hampstead, NH 03826	603-887-2310	webmaster@albinism.org	www.albinism.org
National Organization on Disability (NOD)	910 16ᵗʰ Street NW Suite 600 Washington, DC 20006	202-293-5960	ability@nod.org	www.nod.org
National Organization on Fetal Alcohol Syndrome (NOFAS)	900 17ᵗʰ Street NW Suite 910 Washington, DC 20006	202-785-4585	information@nofas.org	www.nofas.org
National Patient Air Transport Hotline	4620 Haygood Road Suite 1 Virginia Beach, VA 23445	757-318-9174	mercymedical@erols.com	www.patienttravel.org
National Resource Center for Family Centered Practice	100 Oakdale Hall Iowa City IA 52242	319-335-4965	none listed	www.uiowa.edu/~nrcfcp
National Resource Center for Paraprofessionals in Education and Related Services	6526 Old Main Hill Logan, UT 84322	435-797-7272	twallace@nrcpara.org	www.nrcpara.org
National Resource Center on Supported Living and Choice	805 S. Crouse Avenue Syracuse, NY 13244	315-443-3851	thechip@sued.syr.edu	thechp.syr.edu/nrc.html

ORGANIZATION	ADDRESS	TELEPHONE	E-MAIL	WEBSITE
National Reye's Syndrome Foundation	P.O. Box 829 Bryan, OH 43506	419-636-2679	nrsf@reyessyndrome. org	www.reyessyndrome. org
National Scoliosis Foundation	5 Cabot Place Stoughton, MA 02072	781-6333	NSF@scoliosis.org	www.scoliosis.org
National Sleep Foundation	1522 K Street NW Suite 500 Washington, DC 20005	202-347-3471	nsf@sleepfoundation. org	www.sleepfoundation. org
National Spinal Cord Injury Association	6701 Democracy Blvd. Suite 300-9 Bethesda, MD 20817	301-214-4006	info@spinalcord.org	www.spinalcord.org
National Stuttering Association	119 W. 40th Street 14th Floor New York, NY 10018	800-937-8888	info@westutter.org	www.westutter.org
National Tay-Sachs and Allied Diseases Association	2001 Beacon Street Suite 204 Brighton, MA 02135	800-906-8723	info@ntsad.org	www.ntsad.org
Neurofibromatosis, Inc.	9320 Annapolis Road Suite 300 Lanham, MD 20706	301-918-4600	nfinfo@nfinc.org	www.nfinc.org

ORGANIZATION	ADDRESS	TELEPHONE	E-MAIL	WEBSITE
Nonverbal Learning Disorders Association	2446 Albany Avenue West Hartford, CT 06117	800-570-0217	NLDA@nlda.org	www.nlda.org
Obsessive Compulsive Foundation, Inc.	676 State Street New Haven, CT 06511	203-401-2070	info@ocfoundation.org	www.ocfoundation.org
Osteogenesis Imperfecta Foundation	804 Diamond Avenue Suite 210 Gaithersburg, MD 20878	301-947-0083	bonelink@oif.org	www.oif.org
Parents Helping Parents	3041 Olcott Street Santa Clara, CA 95054	408-727-5775	info@php.com	www.php.com
Parents of Galactosemic Children	1519 Magnolia Bluff Dr. Gautier, MS 39553	none listed	president@galactosemia.org	www.galactosemia.org
Pathways Awareness Foundation	150 N. Michigan Avenue Suite 2100 Chicago, IL 60601	800-955-2445	friends@pathwaysawareness.org	www.pathwaysawareness.org
Recording for the Blind and Dyslexic	20 Roszel Road Princeton, NJ 08540	800-221-4792	custserv@rfbd.org	www.rfbd.org
Registry of Interpreters for the Deaf	333 Commerce Street Aleandria, VA 22314	703-838-0030	info@rid..org	www.rid.org

ORGANIZATION	ADDRESS	TELEPHONE	E-MAIL	WEBSITE
RESNA (Rehabilitation Engineering and Assistive Technology Society of North America	1700 N. Moore Street Suite 1540 Arlington, VA 22209	703-524-6686	info@resna.org	www.resna.org
Schwab Learning	1650 S. Amphlett Blvd. Suite 300 San Mateo, CA 94402	650-655-2410	webmaster@ schwablearning.org	www.schwablearning. org
Scleroderma Foundation	12 Kent Way Suite 101 Byfield, MA 01922	978-463-5843	sfinfo@scleroderma.org	www.scleroderma.org
Self Help for Hard of Hearing People, Inc. (SHHH)	7910 Woodmont Avenue Suite 1200 Bethesda, MD 20814	301-657-2248	information@ hearingloss.org	www.hearingloss.org
Special Needs Advocate for Parents (SNAP	11835 W. Olympic Blvd. Suite 465 Los Angeles, Ca 90069	310-479-3755	info@snapinfo.org	www.snapinfo.org
Special Olympics International	1133 19th Street NW Washington, DC 20036	202-628-3630	info@specialolympics. org	www.specialolympics. org
Spina Bifida Association of America	4590 MacArthur Blvd. NW, Suite 250 Washington, DC 20007	202-944-3285	sbaa@sbaa.org	www.sbaa.org

ORGANIZATION	ADDRESS	TELEPHONE	E-MAIL	WEBSITE
Stuttering Foundation	3100 Walnut Grove Road Suite 603 Memphis, Tn 38111	901-452-7343	stutter@stutteringhelp. org	www.stutteringhelp. org
TASH (formerly the Association for Persons with Severe Handicaps)	29 W. Susquehanna Ave. Suite 210 Baltimore, MD 21204	410-828-8274	info@tash.org	www.tash.org
Tourette Syndrome Association	42-40 Bell Boulevard Bayside, NY 11361	718-224-2999	ts@tsa-usa.org	www.tsa-usa.org
Trace R&D Center	1550 Engineering Drive 2107 Engineering Hall Madison, WI 53706	608-262-6966	info@trace.wisc.edu	www.trace.wisc.edu
Tuberous Sclerosis Alliance	801 Roder Road Suite 750 Silver Spring, MD 20910	301-562-9890	info@tsalliance.org	www.tsalliance.org
United Cerebral Palsy Association, Inc.	1660 L Street NW Suite 700 Washington, DC 20036	202-776-0406	national@ucp.org	www.ucp.org
United Leukodystrophy Foundation	2304 Highland Drive Sycamore, IL 60178	800-728-5483	ulf@tbcnet.com	www.ulf.org

ORGANIZATION	ADDRESS	TELEPHONE	E-MAIL	WEBSITE
U.S. Society of Augmentative and Alternative Communication (USSAAC)	P.O. Box 21418 Sarasota, FL 34276	941-925-8875	USSAAC@msn.com	www.ussaac.org
Vestibular Disorders Association	P.O. Box 13305 Portland, OR 97213	503-229-7705	veda@vestibular.org	www.vestibular.org
Williams Syndrome Association, Inc.	P.O. Box 297 Clawson, MI 48017	248-244-2229	info@williams-syndrome.org	www.williams-syndrome.org
World Association of Persons with Disabilities	4503 Sunnyview Drive Suite 112 P.O. Box 14111 Oklahoma City, OK 73135	405-672-4440	thehub@wapd.org	www.wapd.org
Zero to Three National Center for Infants, Toddlers, and Families	2000 M Street NW Suite 200 Washington, DC 20036	202-638-1144	none listed	www.zerotothree.org

APPENDIX 6:
FEDERAL RESOURCE DIRECTORY - ADA
COMPLIANCE INFORMATION

ORGANIZATION	ADDRESS	TELEPHONE	WEBSITE
U.S. Department of Justice - ADA Information Line	U.S. Department of Justice Civil Rights Division Disability Rights Section P.O. Box 66738 Washington, DC 20035	800-514-0301 (voice)800-514-0383 (TDD)	http://www.ada.gov
Equal Employment Opportunity Commission	U.S. Equal Employment Opportunity Commission 1801 L Street NW Washington, DC 20507	800-669-4000 (voice)800-669-6820 (TDD)	http://www.eeoc.gov
U.S. Department of Transportation - ADA Assistance Line	U.S. Department of Transportation Federal Transit Administration 400 Seventh Street SW Washington, DC 20590	888-446-4511 (voice)	http://www.fta.dot. gov/civilrights/civil rights 2360.html

ORGANIZATION	ADDRESS	TELEPHONE	WEBSITE
Federal Communications Commission	Federal Communications Commission 400 Seventh Street SW Washington, DC 20590	888-225-5322 (voice) 888-835-5322 (TTY)	http://www.fcc.gov/cib/dro
Architectural and Transportation Barriers Compliance Board	Architectural and Transportation Barriers Compliance Board 1331 F Street NW Suite 1000 Washington, DC 20004	800-872-2253(voice)/ 800-993-2822 (TTY)	http://www.access-board.gov
U.S. Department of Labor - Job Accommodation Network	Job Accommodation Network P.O. Box 6080 Morgantown, WV 26506	800-526-7234 (voice) 877-781=9403 (TTY)	http://www.jan.wvu.edu
U.S. Department of Education - Regional Disability and Business Technical Assistance Centers	VCU DBTAC Outreach and Research Center 1112 East Clay Street P.O. Box 980330 Richmond, VA 23298	800-949-4232 (voice & TTY)	http://www.adata.org

SOURCE: U.S. Department of Justice

APPENDIX 7:
SETTLEMENT AGREEMENT BETWEEN THE UNITED STATES OF AMERICA AND THE BOARD OF EDUCATION OF THE CITY OF CHICAGO - DISABILITY ACCOMMODATIONS

1. The parties to this Settlement Agreement are the United States of America and the Board of Education of the City of Chicago.

2. In this Agreement the United States Department of Justice is referred to as the "Department"; the Board of Education of the City of Chicago, its agents, employees, officials, and designees, are referred to as the "Board"; Mr. Robert L. Dixon is referred to as "Mr. Dixon"; and the Equal Employment Opportunity Commission is referred to as the "EEOC".

3. Title I of the Americans with Disabilities Act of 1990, as amended, 42 U.S.C. §§ 12111 et seq., is referred to as "title I" or the "ADA."

The parties hereby agree as follows:

JURISDICTION

4. The Board is a person and an employer as defined by title I, Section 101, 42 U.S.C. § 12111(7) and Section 101, 42 U.S.C. § 12111(5)(a) respectively.

5. On December 13, 1993, Mr. Dixon filed a charge with the EEOC alleging that the Board had violated title I of the ADA by refusing to accommodate his disability (arthritis).

6. In his charge Mr. Dixon alleged that the violation occurred on October 13, 1993, and was continuing. Since the charge was filed on December 13, 1993, and within 300 days 1 of the alleged discriminatory act, it is timely.

7. On August 31, 1994, the EEOC issued a letter of determination. The EEOC found reasonable cause to believe that the Board violated title I of the ADA when it denied Mr. Dixon reasonable accommodation to perform the essential functions of his job.

8. After conciliation failed on September 27, 1994, the EEOC, as authorized by Section 107(a) of title I, 42 U.S.C. § 12117(a), referred Mr. Dixon's charge to the Department with a recommendation that a civil action be filed under the ADA.

1 Under Section 706 this is the statutory filing period in states, such as Illinois, which has been designated by the EEOC as a deferral state.

BACKGROUND

9. Mr. Dixon taught various grades at the Joseph Middle School in Chicago since 1954. During the 1993-1994 school year he was assigned to teach a class located on the third floor of the school building.

10. His duties required him to escort his class up and down three flights of stairs to activities (lunch, gym and library) located in the basement of the building.

11. At various times during the fall of 1993 Dixon requested relocation of his class from the third floor to the first or second floor as an accommodation for his disability. Mr. Dixon's requests were not successful.

12. From November 13, 1993 to May 3, 1994, Mr. Dixon used sixty-nine (69) days of sick leave.

13. On April 25, 1994, Mr. Dixon submitted his resignation in order to become eligible for retirement benefits.

14. On May 3, 1994, Mr. Dixon formally retired from his teacher position at Joseph Middle School. On his resignation he noted that the reason he had decided to retire was because his request for relocation of his classroom as an accommodation for his disability was unsuccessful.

15. The United States alleges that the Board violated title I of the ADA, among other ways: by failing or refusing reasonably to accommodate Mr. Dixon's known physical limitations to enable him to perform the essential functions as a school teacher at the Joseph Middle School; by forcing him to take sick leave and eventually forcing him to retire; and

by failing and refusing to take appropriate action to remedy the effects of the discriminatory treatment of Mr. Dixon.

16. The Board denies that any action it has taken constitutes a violation of title I of the ADA. This Agreement shall not be construed as an admission of liability by the Board.

17. The parties have determined that their respective interests can be met without engaging in protracted litigation to resolve this dispute and have therefore voluntarily entered into this Agreement.

GENERAL AGREEMENT

Specific Relief to be Offered by the Board

18. On or before January 8, 1996, the Board will offer a monetary amount of $20,599.22 to Mr. Dixon as compensatory damages for injuries sustained as a result of the Board's actions.

19. The Board's offer to Mr. Dixon will be made in a letter, the contents of which will be the same as in Exhibit 1 (see attached). The offer letter will advise Mr. Dixon that in order to accept the relief offered, he must return a signed and notarized Release, the contents of which will be the same as in Exhibit 2 (see attached), to the Board in care of its counsel within thirty (30) days of his receipt of the offer letter.

20. Mr. Dixon does not seek job relief or reinstatement from the Board and, accordingly, none has been requested by the Department on his behalf.

21. The Board will send to the undersigned counsel for the United States a copy of the offer letter and release that it sends to Mr. Dixon. If Mr. Dixon accepts the Board's offer, the Board will send a copy of the signed and notarized release to the undersigned counsel for the United States.

22. The Board will notify the undersigned counsel for the United States when it has completed the actions described in paragraphs 16-18.

23. Within thirty (30) days of receiving from the Board a copy of the offer letters to be sent to Mr. Dixon by the Board according to this Agreement, the United States will issue to both Mr. Dixon a notice of right to sue on EEOC charge No. 210-94-1285 under Section 107, 42 U.S.C. § 12117(a) and 42 U.S.C. § 2000e-5(f)(1).

IMPLEMENTATION

24. The Attorney General is authorized, by Section 107(a) of title I, 42 U.S.C. § 12117(a), to institute a civil action against a local government employer when the EEOC has determined that there is reasonable cause

to believe that a charge of employment discrimination is true, and the EEOC has been unable to obtain a conciliation agreement. These preconditions exist with respect to EEOC charge No. 210-94-1285. In consideration for the Board's offering relief to Mr. Dixon, as set forth above, the Attorney General will not institute any civil action alleging employment discrimination by the Board on the basis of EEOC charge No. 210-94-1285, filed by Mr. Dixon.

OTHER PROVISIONS

25. The Department of Justice may institute a civil action in the appropriate U.S. District Court to enforce this Agreement, if the Department believes that this Agreement or any requirement thereof has been violated. The Department may review compliance with this Agreement at any time. If the Department believes that this Agreement or any portion of it has been violated, it will raise its concern(s) with the Board and the parties will attempt to resolve the concern(s) in good faith. The Board will be given twenty-one (21) days to cure any breach of this Agreement prior to the institution of any enforcement action.

26. Failure by the Department to enforce this entire Agreement or any of its provision shall not be construed as a waiver of its right to enforce other provisions of this Agreement.

27. A person signing this document in a representative capacity for either party is authorized to bind that party to this Agreement.

28. This Agreement is a public document and constitutes the entire agreement between the parties on this matter. Any statement, promise, or agreement, either written or oral, made by either party or agents of either party, that is not contained or referred in this written Agreement, shall not be enforceable. Copies of this Agreement shall be made available to any person by either party upon request to that party.

EFFECTIVE DATE AND TERMINATION DATE

29. The effective date of this Agreement is the date of the last signature below.

On Behalf of the Chicago
School Reform
Board of Trustees of the Board of
Education of the City of Chicago

By: (Signature)
Attorney

For the United States:

By: (Signature)
Assistant Attorney General
Disability Rights Section
Civil Rights Division

Board of Education of the
City of Chicago
Chicago, IL 60609
Dated:

P.O. Box 66738
Washington, D.C. 20035-6738
(202) 514-3816

EXHIBIT 1

VIA CERTIFIED MAIL,
RETURN RECEIPT REQUESTED
Robert L. Dixon
5050 South Lake Shore Drive
Chicago, IL 60615

Re: Dixon v. Chicago Board of Education
EEOC Charge No. 210-94-1285

Dear Mr. Dixon:

The United States and the Board of Education of the City of Chicago ("Board") have entered into a Settlement Agreement to resolve the above matter. A copy of the Agreement is enclosed.

Under the Agreement, the Board is offering you a monetary amount of $20,599.22, as backpay relief. In order to accept the Board's offer to you, you must sign and notarize the enclosed Release and return it to the Board within thirty (30) days of your receipt of this letter. You may return the Release by mail or in person to:

Assistant Attorney
Board of Education of the Board of Chicago
Law Department-5 (North)
1819 W. Pershing Rd.
Chicago, IL 60609

As set forth in paragraph 19 of the Agreement, the United States will, within thirty (30) days after it receives a copy of this letter, issue to you a notice of your right to sue on EEOC charge No. 210-94-1285. If, however, you accept the relief being offered to you by the Board under this Agreement, and signify you accept the relief offered by executing the enclosed Release, you will thereby agree not to exercise your right to file suit on that charge.

If you have any questions on this Agreement or the Board's offer to you, you may call collect, station-to-station, or write to the following attorney at the U.S. Department of Justice:

Disability Rights Section
Civil Rights Division

U.S. Department of Justice
P.O. Box 66738
Washington, D.C. 20035-6738
(202) 514-3816

Enclosures

EXHIBIT 2

RELEASE OF ALL CLAIMS

For and in consideration of accepting the relief offered to me by the Board of Education of the City of Chicago ("Board"), under a Settlement Agreement between the United States of America and the Board of $20,599.22 as backpay relief and sick pay:

I, Robert Dixon, on behalf of myself, executors, heirs and assigns, release and discharge the Board and its current, former, and future agents, employees, officials, and designees, of and from all legal and equitable claims, known or unknown, arising out of EEOC charge No. 210-94-1285 which I filed with the Chicago Office of the Equal Employment Opportunity Commission on or about December 13, 1993. I further agree that I will not exercise my right to institute against the Board any civil action alleging employment discrimination on the basis of EEOC charge No. 210-94-1285 or any of the facts alleged in the charge.

I understand that the payment that is being offered to me does not constitute an admission by the Board of the validity of any claim raised by me or on my behalf.

This Release constitutes the entire agreement between the Board and myself.

I acknowledge that I am of legal age and under no mental incapacity.

I acknowledge that a copy of the Settlement Agreement between the Board and the United States of America resolving the matter between them has been made available to me.

I HAVE READ THIS RELEASE AND UNDERSTAND ITS THE CONTENTS AND I

SIGN THIS RELEASE OF MY OWN FREE ACT WILL.

Signed this ____ day of _____, ____.

OTHER PROVISIONS

25. The Department of Justice may institute a civil action in the appropriate U.S. District Court to enforce this Agreement, if the Department believes that this Agreement or any requirement thereof has been violated. The Department may review compliance with this Agreement at any time. If the Department believes that this Agreement or any portion of it has been violated, it will raise its concern(s) with the Board and the parties will attempt to resolve the concern(s) in good faith. The Board will be given twenty-one (21) days to cure any breach of this Agreement prior to the institution of any enforcement action.

26. Failure by the Department to enforce this entire Agreement or any of its provision shall not be construed as a waiver of its right to enforce other provisions of this Agreement.

27. A person signing this document in a representative capacity for either party is authorized to bind that party to this Agreement.

28. This Agreement is a public document and constitutes the entire agreement between the parties on this matter. Any statement, promise, or agreement, either written or oral, made by either party or agents of either party, that is not contained or referred in this written Agreement, shall not be enforceable. Copies of this Agreement shall be made available to any person by either party upon request to that party.

EFFECTIVE DATE AND TERMINATION DATE

29. The effective date of this Agreement is the date of the last signature below.

On Behalf of the Chicago
School Reform
Board of Trustees of the Board of
Education of the City of Chicago

By: (Signature)
Attorney
Board of Education of the
City of Chicago
Chicago, IL 60609
Dated:

For the United States:

By: (Signature)
Assistant Attorney General
Disability Rights Section
Civil Rights Division
P.O. Box 66738
Washington, D.C. 20035-6738
(202) 514-3816

APPENDIX 8:
DIRECTORY OF STATE GOVERNORS' COMMITTEES ON EMPLOYMENT OF THE DISABLED

STATE	DEPARTMENT	ADDRESS	TELEPHONE	FAX	WEBSITE
Alabama	Governor's Committee on Employment of People with Disabilities, Department of Rehabilitation Service	P.O. Box 698 Dothan, AL 36302	334-699-8600	334-792-1783	none listed
Alaska	Governor's Committee on Employment of People with Disabilities	801 W. 10th Street, Suite A Juneau, AK 99801	907-465-6922	907-465-2856	www.labor. state.ak.us/ govscomm/ home.htm
Arizona	Governor's Committee on Employment of People with Disabilities	P.O. Box 16404 Phoenix, AZ 85011	602-266-6752	602-241-7158	none listed

STATE	DEPARTMENT	ADDRESS	TELEPHONE	FAX	WEBSITE
Arkansas	Governor's Commission on People with Disabilities	P.O. Box 3781 1616 Brookwood Drive Little Rock, AR 72202	501-296-1637	501-296-1883	none listed
California	Governor's Committee for Employment of Disabled Persons	P.O. Box 826880 722 Capitol Mall, Rm. 3099 Sacramento, CA 94280	916-654-8055	916-654-9821	www.edd. ca.gov/gcepdind. asp
Colorado	Department of Human Services, Disability Determination Services	2530 South Parker Road Aurora, CO 80014	303-368-4100	303-752-5692	www.cdhs.state. co.us/dds
Connecticut	Governor's Committee on Employment of People with Disabilities	200 Folly Brook Boulevard Wethersfield, CT 06109	302-761-8275	302-761-6611	none listed
Delaware	Governor's Committee on Employment of People with Disabilities	4425 North Market Street P.O. Box 9969 Wilmington, DE 19809	302-761-8275	302-761-6611	none listed
District of Columbia	Mayor's Committee on Persons with Disabilities	810 First Street NE Room 10015 Washington, DC 20002	202-442-8673	202-442-8742	none listed
Florida	The Able Trust/Florida Governor's Alliance	106 East College Avenue Suite 820 Tallahassee, FL 32301	850-224-4493	850-224-4496	www.abletrust. org

STATE	DEPARTMENT	ADDRESS	TELEPHONE	FAX	WEBSITE
Georgia	Committee on Employment of People with Disabilities, Inc.	P.O. Box 1090 Fortson, GA 31808	706-595-3768	706-324-4549	LeeAmiller@att.net
Hawaii	Disability and Communication Access Board	919 Ala Moana Boulevard Suite 101 Honolulu, HI 96814	808-586-8121	808-586-8129	www.hawaii.gov/health/dcab/home/index.htm
Idaho	Governor's Committee on Employment of People with Disabilities	317 Main Street Boise, ID 83735	208-332-3750	208-327-7331	none listed
Illinois	DHS/Office of Rehabilitation Services	100 West Randolph Street Suite 5-300 Chicago, IL 60601	312-814-4036	312-814-5849	www.dhs.state.il.us/ors
Indiana	Governor's Planning Council for People with Disabilities	143 West Market StreetIndianapolis, IN 46204	317-232-7770	317-232-3712	www.in.gov/gpcpd
Iowa	Commission of Persons with Disabilities - Department of Human Rights	Lucas State Office Building 321 East 12th StreetDes Moines, IA 50319	515-242-6334	515-242-6119	www.state.ia.us/government/dhr/pd
Kansas	Kansas Commission on Disability Concerns	1000 SW Jackson Suite 100 Topeka, KS 66612	800-295-5232	785-296-6809	http://kdoch.state.ks.us/KCDC

STATE	DEPARTMENT	ADDRESS	TELEPHONE	FAX	WEBSITE
Kentucky	Office of the Kentucky ADA Coordinator	500 Mero Street, 2nd Floor Frankfort, KY 40601	502-564-5331	502-564-7799	none listed
Louisiana	Governor's Advisory Council on Disability Affairs	P.O. Box 94004 Baton Rouge, LA 70801	225-219-7550	225-668-2722	http://gov. louisiana. gov/disabilityaffairs
Maine	Commission on Disability and Employment	P.O. Box 9715, Suite 178 Portland, ME 04101	207-626-2774	none listed	none listed
Maryland	Department of Disabilities	217 E. Redwood Suite 1301 Baltimore, MD 21202	410-767-3660	410-333-6674	www.mdtap.org
Massachusetts	Governor's Commission on Employment of People with Disabilities	19 Stanford Street, 3rd Floor Boston, MA 02114	617-626-5239	617-727-0315	none listed
Michigan	Commission on Disability Concerns	201 N. Washington Square Suite 150 Lansing, MI 48913	517-335-0103	517-335-7773	www.michigan. gov
Minnesota	State Council on Disability	121 E. 7th Place Suite 107St. Paul, MN 55101	651-296-1743	651-296-5935	www.state. mn.us

STATE	DEPARTMENT	ADDRESS	TELEPHONE	FAX	WEBSITE
Mississippi	Department of Rehabilitation Services	P.O. Box 1698, Jackson, MS 39215	601-853-5200	601-853-5205	www.mdrs. state.ms.us
Missouri	Governor's Council on Disability	P.O. Box 1668 301 West High Street Suite 250-A Jefferson City, MO 65102	573-751-2600	573-526-4109	www.gcd.oa.mo. gov
Montana	Governor's Disabilities Advisory Council	P.O. Box 4210 Helena, MT 59504	406-444-0062	406-444-1971	none listed
Nebraska	Department of Workforce Development	P.O. Box 94600 Lincoln, NE 68509	402-471-1050	402-471-2318	www.Nebraska Workforce.com
Nevada	State Rehabilitation Council	1370 S. Curry Street Carson City, NV 89703	775-684-4199	775-684-4186	www.nvdetr.org
Newhampshire	Governor's Commission on Disability	57 Regional Drive,Concord, NH 03301	603-271-2773	603-271-2837	www. nh.gov/disability
New Jersey	Department of Labor	P.O. Box 398 Trenton, NJ 08625	609-292-7959	609-292-8347	www.state.nj. us/labor/dvrs/ vrsindex.html
New Mexico	Governor's Commission on Disability	491 Old Santa Fe Trail Room 117 Santa Fe, NM 87501	505-476-0412	505-827-6328	http://gcd.state. nm.us

STATE	DEPARTMENT	ADDRESS	TELEPHONE	FAX	WEBSITE
New York	Commission on Quality Care and Advocacy for Persons with Disabilities	401 State Street Schenectady, NY 12305	518-388-1281	518-388-2860	www.cqc.state.ny.us
North Carolina	Governor's Advocacy Council for Persons with Disabilities	1314 Mail Service Center Raleigh, NC 27699	919-733-9250	919-733-9173	www.gacpd.com
Northdakota	Human Services - Disability Services Division	1237 W. Divide Avenue Suite 1A Bismarck, ND 58501	701-328-8958	701-328-8969	www.nd.gov/humanservices/services/disabilities/index.html
Ohio	Governor's Council on People with Disabilities	400 East Campus View Boulevard Columbus, OH 43235	614-438-1393	614-438-1274	www.gcpd.ohio.gov
Oklahoma	Office of Handicapped Concerns	2401 NW 23rd Street Suite 90 Oklahoma City, OK 73107	405-521-3756	405-522-6695	www.ohc.ok.gov
Oregon	Disabilities Commission	676 Church Street NE Salem, OR 97301	503-378-3142	503-378-7615	www.oregon.gov/DHS/odhhs
Pennsylvania	Governor's Committee on Employment of People with Disabilities	1521 North Sixth Street Harrisburg, PA 17102	717-772-6382	717-783-5221	www.dli.state.pa.us

STATE	DEPARTMENT	ADDRESS	TELEPHONE	FAX	WEBSITE
Rhode Island	Governor's Commission on Disabilities	41 Cherry Dale Court Cranston, RI 02920	401-462-0100	401-462-0106	www. disabilities. ri.gov
South Carolina	Vocational Rehabilitation Department	1410 Boston Avenue P.O. Box 15West Columbia, SC 29171	803-896-6500	none listed	www.scvrd.net
South Dakota	Board of Vocational Rehabilitation	221 South Central Avenue Pierre, SD 57501	605-945-2207	605-945-2422	none listed
Tennessee	Committee for Employment of People with Disabilities	400 Deaderick Street Nashville, TN 37248	615-313-4891	615-741-6508	http://tennessee. gov/humanserv/ rehab/cc5.htm
Texas	Governor's Committee on People with Disabilities	P.O. Box 12428 Austin, TX 78711	512-463-5742	512-463-5745	www.governor. state. tx.us/disabilities
Utah	Governor's Committee on Employment of People with Disabilities	1595 West 500 South Salt Lake City, UT 84104	801-887-9392	801-887-9389	none listed
Vermont	Governor's Committee on Employment of People with Disabilities	P.O. Box 748 Richmond, VT 05477	802-434-6600	802-329-2191	www.hireus.org
Virginia	Board of People with Disabilities	202 North 9th Street 9th Floor Richmond, VA 23219	804-786-0016	804-786-1118	www.vaboard. org

STATE	DEPARTMENT	ADDRESS	TELEPHONE	FAX	WEBSITE
Washington	Governor's Committee on Disability Issues and Employment	P.O. Box 9046 Olympia, WA 98507	360-438-3168	360-438-3208	http://fortress.wa.gov/esd/portal/gcde
West Virginia	Division of Rehabilitation Services	State Capitol Complex P.O. Box 50890, Charleston, WV 25305	304-766-4601	304-766-4905	www.wvdrs.org
Wisconsin	Governor's Committee for People with Disabilities	P.O. Box 7850 Madison, WI 53707	608-266-7974	608-266-3386	http://dhfs.wisconsin.gov/disabilities/physical/gcpd.htm
Wyoming	Governor's Committee for People with Disabilities	1100 Herschler Building 1st Floor - East Wing Cheyenne, WY 82002	307-777-7191	307-777-7155	http://wyomingworkforce.org/who/disabled.aspx

SOURCE: U.S. Department of Labor

APPENDIX 9:
DISCRIMINATION COMPLAINT FORM - TITLE II OF THE ADA

U.S. Department of Justice
Civil Rights Division
Disability Rights Section

OMB No. 1190-0009 Exp. Date 04/30/2007

Title II of the Americans with Disabilities Act
Section 504 of the Rehabilitation Act of 1973
Discrimination Complaint Form

Instructions: Please fill out this form completely, in black ink or type. Sign and return to the address on page 3.

Complainant:

Address:

City, State and Zip Code:

Telephone: Home:

      Business:

Person Discriminated Against:
(if other than the complainant)

Address:

City, State, and Zip Code:

Telephone: Home:

      Business:

Government, or organization, or institution which you believe has discriminated:

DISCRIMINATION COMPLAINT FORM - TITLE II OF THE ADA

Name: _____

Address: _____

County: _____

City: _____

State and Zip Code: _____

Telephone Number: _____

When did the discrimination occur? Date: _____

Describe the acts of discrimination providing the name(s) where possible of the individuals who
discriminated (use space on page 3 if necessary): _____

_____

_____

Have efforts been made to resolve this complaint through the internal grievance procedure of the
government, organization, or institution?

Yes_____ No_____

If yes: what is the status of the grievance? _____

_____

_____

Has the complaint been filed with another bureau of the Department of Justice or any other Federal, State, or
local civil rights agency or court?

Yes_____ No_____

If yes:

Agency or Court: _____

Contact Person: _____

Address: _____

City, State, and Zip Code: _____

Telephone Number: _____

Date Filed: _____

Do you intend to file with another agency or court?

       Yes_____ No_____

Agency or Court: _____

Address: _____

City, State and Zip Code: _____

Telephone Number: _____

Additional space for answers:

_____

_____

_____

_____

_____

_____

Signature: _____

Date: _____

Return to:

U.S. Department of Justice
Civil Rights Division
950 Pennsylvania Avenue, NW
Disability Rights - NYAV
Washington, D.C. 20530

last updated April 29, 2005

APPENDIX 10:
SETTLEMENT AGREEMENT BETWEEN THE UNITED STATES OF AMERICA AND WALT DISNEY WORLD CO. - AUXILIARY AIDS

This Agreement between Walt Disney World Co. (WDW) and the United States Department of Justice (Department) is the culmination of an on-going and mutually beneficial process to make WDW more accessible to persons with hearing impairments.

The background and procedure that has led to this agreement is both illuminating and instructive in terms of the benefits to be derived from collaborative efforts between private industry and the government. Prior to the enactment of the Americans with Disabilities Act (ADA) and its effective date in 1992, WDW was committed to meeting the needs of its guests with disabilities, and had been recognized as an innovator in that regard. With respect to hearing-related disabilities, WDW has offered to guests who are deaf or hard of hearing a variety of auxiliary aides, including assistive listening systems, TDDs, captioning on television, and written aides to communication at many of its shows and attractions.

Following enactment of the ADA, the Department advised WDW that some guests with hearing disabilities claimed that they were denied effective communication as required by the ADA. As a result of the concerns addressed by the Department which have since been resolved separately, the Department proceeded to investigate and began an ongoing discussion with WDW. Together, with the Department's assistance, WDW has undertaken a variety of innovative steps to better address the needs of persons who are deaf or hard of hearing.

While WDW is committed to continuing its exploration of new and improved methods and services, the following represents an agreement between WDW and the Department as to effective communication at this time:

1. WDW agrees to continue to provide those auxiliary aids and services necessary for deaf and hearing-impaired individuals to enjoy the programs and services at the Walt Disney World Resort, in accordance with 42 U.S.C. §12182(b)(2)(A)(iii). While methods of complying with the ADA will differ depending upon the particular attraction, such methods include, but are not limited to: captioning; sign language interpreters; assistive listening systems (ALS); and written aids. This Agreement provides for specific auxiliary aids for each attraction at Walt Disney World as identified in Attachment A, which is incorporated in this Agreement by reference. WDW's efforts to develop other effective auxiliary aids will continue to evolve.

2. a. WDW shall make interpreting services available at the Magic Kingdom, Epcot, and Disney-MGM Studios on a rotating scheduled basis so that guests will know precisely when those services are available at the specific park. WDW's interpreters will be qualified sign language interpreters capable of oral or ASL interpretations. The schedule will alternate at each of the three parks in rotation so that one performance of each identified show will be interpreted on the day scheduled for interpreting, timed to permit guests to attend all the interpreted shows at that park on that day. Guests with hearing disabilities who wish to see those interpreted performances must notify WDW Guest Services at least fourteen (14) days prior to the day and date upon which services are to be scheduled. In special circumstances, such as a visit of three days or less when interpreting is not available at the guest's park of choice, WDW shall also make an effort to provide interpreter services on a day on which they are not regularly scheduled. It is the parties' hope and expectation that the two-week notice requirement will be reduced to one week, or less, no later than December 31, 1998, unless WDW informs the Department on or before November 1, 1998, that there is good cause for not being able to shorten the two week notice provision.

2. b. Guests who wish to request interpreted performances of: (i) Epcot World Showcase street-type entertainers; (ii) America Gardens performances; or (iii) House of Invention, none of which will appear on the interpreter schedule must request the interpreter services at least 14 days prior to the date on which they would like the services. Among these events, which may change from time to time, are currently

included: Voices of Liberty; Le Clown Gordoon; Jon Armstrong Magic Show; Pam Brody; World Showcase Players; Canadian Comedy Corps.

2. c. Guests requiring interpreter services shall identify themselves to WDW personnel at the attraction scheduled for interpreting and the guest and one companion shall be provided seating that will permit them to see the interpreter without obstacles or interference during the attraction or event.

2. d. WDW will of course impose no surcharge on persons with disabilities to cover the cost of providing any auxiliary aids, in accordance with 42 U.S.C. §12182(b)(2)(A)(i).

2. e. Printed interpreter schedules will be available at all Guest Services locations. Interpreter information is also available from Guest Services by telephone and on the WDW site on the Internet.

3. WDW has been working on developing discrete captioning for attractions at Walt Disney World for a number of years. As a result of those efforts and the Department's assistance, WDW can and will provide captioning services at various attractions as set forth on Attachment A. These services shall be available regardless of date or time and without advance notice requirements. Any guest may obtain information regarding captioning services and any auxiliary aids or devices at Guest Services locations.

4. For those attractions at which interpreters or captioning are not currently provided under this Agreement, WDW will continue to evaluate and develop technologies or other methods of providing more effective communication for hard of hearing or deaf guests. In the interim, where written aids are the only auxiliary aid presently available, hard of hearing or deaf guests and a companion shall be allowed to experience the ride or attraction a second time promptly, being seated by WDW personnel at the next available performance or rotation of the attraction, if they identify themselves as a person with a hearing disability at the entrance to the ride or attraction.

5. WDW shall promote the availability of its services for persons who are deaf or hard of hearing in print and other marketing media. The parties recognize that publication of the availability of the services for its deaf and hard of hearing guests, as well as the interpreter schedules, is essential to this Agreement. WDW agrees to make one distribution of information about the availability of its services for deaf and hard of hearing persons to major organizations for the deaf and hard of hearing communities, identified by the Department, within a reasonable time following the date of this Agreement.

6. As the parties have discussed, as part of WDW's ongoing efforts, WDW shall continue to evaluate the effectiveness of auxiliary aids and explore methods and technologies in a wide variety of areas including those where WDW is, or will be, providing interpreters or captions. In that regard, WDW shall notify the Department every six months as to any changes and developments in the types of auxiliary aids provided until December 1, 2000, and the parties will cooperate towards determining whether captioning or interpreters are feasible and acceptable for any WDW attraction where they are not already provided on that date.

7. WDW is expanding the scope and depth of employee training in disability awareness, etiquette, and services available, consistent with the employee's responsibilities. Such training includes, as applicable, treatment of guests with disabilities, the availability of services and auxiliary aids, and procedures and policies regarding guests with disabilities. WDW will continue to improve upon the training and training techniques and consider new and better ways of informing its' cast members in this area whenever possible. WDW shall provide training materials to the Department for periodic review, upon request from the Department.

8. WDW will continue to provide a complaint procedure for guests including complaints regarding treatment of guests with hearing disabilities and availability of auxiliary aids. All WDW Guest Services employees located at any Guest Services location shall be trained to respond to questions or complaints about: current policies for addressing the needs of guests with disabilities, information about available transcripts, paper and pencil, and emergency procedures for persons who are deaf or hard of hearing.

9. WDW will conform the aids and services at the Disneyland attractions comparable to those at Walt Disney World identified on Attachment A.

10. The parties understand that nothing contained in this Agreement limits in any way the Department's ability to enforce the ADA against WDW in the future should it not be in compliance with the ADA. Nor does it limit, in any way, WDW's ability to assert any legal defenses available to such claims. Also, by not seeking enforcement of any specific term of this Agreement, neither the Department nor WDW shall have waived its rights, to enforce any other portion of this Agreement. This Agreement does not compromise WDW's continuing obligation to comply with all aspects of the ADA.

11. This Agreement is a public document. Copies of this document, attachments, exhibits, and any information contained in them may be

made available to any person at any time. The Department shall provide copies of these documents to any person upon request.

12. This Agreement fully and accurately reflects the agreement of the signers and no other statement, promise, or agreement, either written or oral, made by either party that is not contained in this written agreement, shall be enforceable.

13. This Agreement shall be effective as of the date set forth below, and it shall be binding on WDW and its successors in interest. WDW will notify any such successors in interest.

APPENDIX 11:
SETTLEMENT AGREEMENT BETWEEN THE UNITED STATES OF AMERICA AND BUDGET-RENT-A CAR SYSTEMS, INC. - PUBLIC ACCOMMODATIONS

A. BACKGROUND

1. This action was initiated by three Complaints filed with the United States Department of Justice ("the Department") against Budget Rent a Car Systems, Inc. ("Budget"). The Complaints were investigated by the Department under the authority granted by Section 308(b) of the Americans with Disabilities Act of 1990 ("ADA"), 42 U.S.C. & § 12188. Two of the Complaints allege that Budget violated the ADA because its policies prohibited persons who are unable to drive due to a disability from renting vehicles even when they were accompanied by licensed drivers. The third Complaint alleges that Budget violated the ADA when its airport shuttle bus driver refused to allow three blind customers accompanied by guide dogs to board the shuttle bus unless the dogs were restrained in kennels.

2. The parties to this Agreement have agreed to forego litigation on the claims presented in these matters and to resolve them as set forth below.

3. The parties to this settlement agreement ("Agreement") are the United States of America and Budget.

B. TITLE III COVERAGE

4. Budget is a public accommodation as defined in section 301(7)(e) of the ADA, 42 U.S.C. §12181, and its implementing regulation, 28 C.F.R. §36.104. In part, the ADA requires public accommodations to make

reasonable modifications to their policies and practices as necessary to afford their goods and services to persons with disabilities, as long as doing so does not fundamentally alter the nature of their goods and services, 42 U.S.C. § 12182(b)(2)(A)(ii) and 28 C.F.R.§ 36.302.

5. The subject of this settlement agreement is the modification of rental policies nationwide by Budget to permit persons who are unable to drive to rent vehicles when they are accompanied by licensed drivers and the modification of policies to provide services to persons with disabilities who use service animals.

6. The Department initiated an investigation of Budget's policy affecting non-driving renters after receiving a Complaint dated October 7, 1992, from a person who has a visual impairment and is unable to drive, alleging that Budget would not allow him to rent a vehicle to be driven by an accompanying licensed driver (Case file DJ 202-79-16). The Department received a similar Complaint on November 12, 1993 (Case file DJ 202-79-42). In November 1995, the Department received a Complaint regarding the treatment of persons with disabilities who are accompanied by service animals (Case file DJ 202-79-50).

7. As described below, Budget has now agreed to modify its policies and procedures. These modifications to Budget's rental policies and procedures are necessary to afford services to individuals with disabilities; the modifications are reasonable and do not fundamentally alter the nature of the services provided by Budget.

C. ACTIONS TO BE TAKEN BY BUDGET

8. In order to afford services to people with disabilities, Budget agrees to nationwide implementation of the following rental policies within 30 days of the date of this agreement.

9. For individuals who are unable to drive due to a physical or mental disability, Budget will not require that the method of payment and driver's license belong to the same individual. All persons who wish to be renters must have the capacity to enter into contracts.

10. Budget may require the authorized driver ("driver") to present a valid driver's license and otherwise meet driver qualification requirements imposed by Budget on its authorized drivers generally, such as minimum age requirements and the customer with a disability ("renter") to present a qualified method of payment and otherwise meet credit qualification requirements imposed by Budget on its renters generally. Renters need not show valid driver's licenses. Budget may require the renter to present some form of photo identification to ensure that he or she is in fact the same person authorized to use a specific method of

payment (cash qualification or credit card). Budget may not require the renter to document that he or she has a disability and may not inquire into the nature or severity of the disability. Budget may, however, require the renter to identify himself or herself as a person with a disability in order to qualify for this procedure. The renter must be required to sign the rental contract. Each person who is permitted to drive the vehicle may be required to be present at the time the vehicle is rented, may be required to present a valid driver's license, may be required to sign the rental agreement solely in the capacity as authorized driver or as an additional authorized driver, as applicable, may be required to submit to a driver's license history check, where applicable, and otherwise meet driver qualification requirements imposed by Budget on its authorized drivers generally.

11. Budget shall waive any "additional driver" charges for one person accompanying a renter with a disability that would otherwise apply, and shall not impose any other surcharge on the renter in connection with actions required by this policy.

12. Budget shall allow persons with disabilities the use of service animals under the ADA, including guide dogs, signal dogs, or other animals individually trained to do work or perform tasks for the benefit of an individual with a disability. Budget shall not require people with disabilities to provide any type of identification or certification of an animal as having been trained as a service animal. Budget shall not require persons with disabilities to be separated from their service animals at any time.

13. Budget shall make available to those individuals who have vision impairments or who are otherwise unable to read the rental contract at time of rental an alternative means of access to the contract terms (e.g., a live reader).

14. Budget shall inform all employees who have contact with the public of the rental policies as described above, and shall remind all such employees on an annual basis for the four years following the effective date of this Agreement. Budget shall incorporate the policies into all appropriate training manuals and programs for employees.

15. All prospective renters, upon request, shall be advised of Budget's rental policies as described above.

16. Budget shall notify all current Licensees of the U.S. Budget Rent a Car Systems of the rental policies as described above, and shall urge current Licensees to adopt those policies. This notification shall consist of distributing the Announcement that is attached hereto as Exhibit A

to all Licensees within thirty (30) days of the effective date of this Agreement. Within ten (10) days of the effective date of each such contract, Budget will distribute this Announcement to all new or renewing Licensees entering into licensing contracts with Budget.

17. Budget shall pay $6,000 in total damages to the three complainants as a group who filed DJ 202-79-50. Budget shall not pay damages to the complainants who filed DJ 202-79-16 and DJ 202-79-42.

D. IMPLEMENTATION AND ENFORCEMENT OF THE SETTLEMENT AGREEMENT

18. Under Section 308(b)(1)(B) of the ADA, 42 U.S.C. §12188(b)(1)(B), the Attorney General is authorized to bring a civil action under title III in any situation where a pattern or practice of discrimination is believed to exist or where a matter of general public importance is raised. In consideration of this Agreement as set forth above, the Attorney General agrees to refrain from undertaking further investigation or from filing civil suit under title III in these matters.

19. The Department may review compliance with this agreement within four years of the date of this Agreement. If the Department believes that this Agreement or any requirement thereof has been violated, it may institute a civil action in the Federal district court for the District of Columbia, or any other appropriate federal district court. A violation of this Agreement shall be deemed a violation of the ADA. 42 U.S.C. §12188(b)(3) and 28 C.F.R. §36.504(b). If the United States demonstrates to a court of competent jurisdiction that such violation has occurred, each individual identified by the United States as aggrieved by the violation shall be compensated by Budget in an amount of no less than $5,000. The United States may also seek civil penalties and other appropriate relief as authorized by the ADA.

20. This Agreement is a public document. A copy of this document or any information contained herein may be made available to any person. Budget or the Department shall provide a copy of this Agreement to any person upon request.

21. This Agreement shall become effective as of the date of the last signature below. This Agreement shall be binding on Budget and its successors in interest. The owners and operators of Budget have a duty to so notify all such successors in interest.

22. This Agreement constitutes the entire agreement between the parties on the matters raised herein, and no other statement, promise, or agreement, either written or oral, made by either party or agents of either party, that is not contained in this written Agreement shall be

enforceable. This Agreement does not purport to remedy any other violations of the ADA or any other federal law other than those specifically addressed herein. This Agreement does not affect Budget's continuing responsibility to comply with all aspects of the ADA.

23. A signatory to this document in a representative capacity for a partnership, corporation, or other such entity represents that he or she is authorized to bind such partnership, corporation, or other entity to this Agreement.

APPENDIX 12:
SETTLEMENT AGREEMENT BETWEEN THE UNITED STATES OF AMERICA AND SHONEY'S INC. - SERVICE ANIMAL

DEPARTMENT OF JUSTICE COMPLAINT NUMBER 202-72-58

BACKGROUND

1. This matter was initiated by a complaint filed under title III of the Americans with Disabilities Act of 1990 ("ADA"), 42 U.S.C. §§ 12181-12189, with the United States Department of Justice ("Department") against Shoney's LLC, the owners and operators of the Shoney's Restaurant ("Restaurant"), located at 2303 Carmack Boulevard, Columbia, Tennessee. The complainants, an individual with a disability and her husband, allege that on May 21, 2005, they were told to leave the Restaurant because they were accompanied by a service animal.

2. The ADA requires that public accommodations make reasonable modifications in policies, practices, and procedures to permit the use of service animals by people with disabilities. 42 U.S.C. § 12182(b)(2)(A)(ii); 28 C.F.R. § 36.302(c).

3. Shoney's, LLC, agrees to modify its policies and practices, as outlined in this Settlement Agreement ("Agreement"), to ensure that individuals who use service animals have an opportunity to use the services provided by the Restaurant that is equal to that of others.

JURISDICTION

4. The Restaurant is an establishment serving food or drink and, as such, is a place of public accommodation. 42 U.S.C. § 12181(7)(B); 28 C.F.R. § 36.104. Shoney's, LLC, owns and operates the Restaurant and,

---

as such, is a public accommodation covered by title III of the ADA. 28 C.F.R. § 36.104.5. The Attorney General is authorized under section 308 of the ADA, 42 U.S.C. §12188, to investigate complaints and bring a civil action under title III in any situation where a pattern or practice of discrimination is believed to exist or where a matter of general public importance is raised.

5. The parties to the Agreement are the Department and Shoney's, LLC. In light of this Agreement, the parties have determined that Department of Justice complaint 202-72-58 can be resolved without litigation and have prepared and agreed to the terms of this Settlement Agreement.

6. In consideration of the terms of this Agreement, the Attorney General agrees to refrain from undertaking further investigation or filing a civil suit in this matter regarding the areas covered under the Remedial Action section of this Agreement, except as provided in the Enforcement and Implementation sections of the Agreement.

REMEDIAL ACTION

7. As soon as practicable, but in no event more than thirty days (30) from the effective date of the Agreement, Shoney's, LLC, agrees to do the following:

8. Shoney's, LLC, shall post the following notice, in 24 font print or larger, in a conspicuous place in the Restaurant:

9. "Individuals with disabilities and their service animals are welcome at Shoney's Restaurants." (Attached hereto as Exhibit A.)

10. Shoney's, LLC, shall adopt and distribute to all its employees at the Restaurant its revised Policy Regarding Service Animals for Customers with Disabilities (attached hereto as Exhibit B). Shoney's, LLC, shall train the Restaurant's current employees as to their obligations under the ADA with respect to service animals so as to ensure that persons with disabilities accompanied by service animals have access to its Restaurant equal to persons without disabilities. Furthermore, during the life of the Agreement, employees hired by Shoney's, LLC, to work at the Restaurant shall be trained and informed of the Restaurant's service animal policy within 24 hours of hire.

11. Shoney's, LLC, within sixty (60) days of the effective date of this Agreement, shall submit a written report with photographs to the Department outlining its compliance with Paragraph 9, above.

ENFORCEMENT

12. If at any time Shoney's, LLC, desires to modify any portion of this Agreement because of changed conditions making performance impossible or impractical or for any other reason, it will promptly notify the Department in writing, setting forth the facts and circumstances thought to justify modification and the substance of the proposed modification. Until there is written Agreement by the Department to the proposed modification, the proposed modification will not take effect. These actions must receive the prior written approval of the Department, which approval shall not be unreasonably withheld or delayed.

13. The Department may review compliance with this Agreement at any time. If the Department believes that Shoney's, LLC, has failed to comply in a timely manner with any requirement of this Agreement without obtaining sufficient advance written agreement with the Department for a modification of the relevant terms, the Department will so notify Shoney's, LLC, in writing and it will attempt to resolve the issue or issues in good faith. If the Department is unable to reach a satisfactory resolution of the issue or issues raised within thirty (30) days of the date it provides notice to Shoney's, LLC, it may institute a civil action in federal district court to enforce the terms of this Agreement or title III and may, in such action, seek any relief available under law.

14. For purposes of the immediately preceding paragraph, it is a violation of this Agreement for Shoney's, LLC, to fail to comply in a timely manner with any of its requirements without obtaining sufficient advance written Agreement with the Department for an extension of the relevant time frame imposed by the Agreement.

15. Failure by the Department to enforce this entire Agreement or any of its provisions or deadlines shall not be construed as a waiver of the Department's right to enforce other deadlines and provisions of this Agreement.

16. This Agreement shall be binding on Shoney's, LLC, its agents and employees. In the event Shoney's, LLC, seeks to transfer or assign all or part of its interest in any facility covered by this Agreement, and the successor or assign intends on carrying on the same or similar use of the facility, as a condition of sale Shoney's, LLC, shall obtain the written accession of the successor or assign to any obligations remaining under this Agreement for the remaining term of this Agreement.

IMPLEMENTATION

17. The effective date of this Agreement is the date of the last signature below.

18. This Agreement, including Exhibits A and B, constitutes the entire Agreement between the parties on the matters raised herein, and no other statement, promise, or agreement, either written or oral, made by either party or agents of either party, that is not contained in this written Agreement, will be enforceable under its provisions.

19. This Agreement is limited to the facts set forth above and does not purport to remedy any other potential violations of the ADA or any other Federal law.

20. This Agreement does not affect Shoney's, LLC's continuing responsibility to comply with all aspects of title III of the ADA. In particular, title III imposes an obligation to make reasonable modifications in policies, practices, or procedures, when the modifications are necessary to afford goods, services, and facilities to individuals with disabilities. This obligation must be continuously re-visited, particularly where the financial resources available to a public accommodation may improve over time.

21. A copy of this document or any information contained in it will be made available to any person by Shoney's, LLC, or the Department upon request.

22. This Agreement will remain in effect for two (2) years from the effective date of this Agreement, or until the parties agree that full compliance with the Agreement by Shoney's, LLC, has been achieved, whichever is later.

23. The person signing this document for Shoney's, LLC, represents that he/she is authorized to bind Shoney's, LLC, to this Agreement.

FOR THE UNITED STATES:

CRAIG S. MORTON
United States Attorney
Middle District of Tennessee

By: (Signature)
MICHAEL L. RODEN
Assistant United States Attorney
B.P.R. No. 010595
Suite A-961

110 Ninth Avenue South

Nashville, TN 37203
Telephone: 615/736-5151

JOHN L. WODATCH, Chief
U.S. Department of Justice
Civil Rights Division
]950 Pennsylvania Avenue, N.W.
Disability Rights Section - NYA
Washington, DC 20530
Date: 12-18-06

FOR THE RESPONDENT:

By: (Signature)
Attorney for Shoney's, LLC

EXHIBIT A

SHONEY'S, INC. CORPORATE POLICY

I PURPOSE/POLICY

In accordance with the Americans with Disabilities Act of 1990, the purpose of this policy is to ensure that all individuals with disabilities, including those requiring the use of service animals, are treated in a non-discriminatory manner and are provided the same level of service and courtesy as all other Customers who visit Shoney's, Inc. restaurants.

II EMPLOYEES COVERED BY THE POLICY

All Employees of Shoney's, Inc. and its affiliated entities (the "Company")

III RESPONSIBILITY FOR ADMINISTRATION

It is the responsibility of all levels of Operations Management and the Human Resources department to administer this policy.

IV PROCEDURES

A. Service animals are animals that are individually trained to perform tasks for people with disabilities. Service animals come in all breeds and sizes, may be trained either by an organization or by an individual with a disability, need not be certified or licensed, and provide a wide range of services that may or may not be identifiable, such as guiding people who are blind, alerting people who are deaf, pulling wheelchairs, alerting and protecting a person who is having a seizure, or performing other special tasks. Service animals are working animals, not pets.

1. If a Shoney's, Inc. employee is unsure that an animal accompanying an individual with a disability is a service animal, Shoney's, Inc. a Restaurant Manager or General Manager may inquire, as discreetly as possible, of any person or group entering the restaurant accompanied by an animal whether it is a service animal required because of a disabilities.

When making such inquiries, keep in mind these guidelines:

EXHIBIT B

A. Exercise careful and good judgment in determining whether there is any need to question the Customer and only do so when uncertain as to the animal's status as a service animal needed because of a disability;
B. Any discussions with a Customer must be conducted by a

B. Restaurant Manager or General Manager and in such a manner so as to avoid any possible embarrassment to the Customer;

C. If you are unsure if the animal is a service animal, the Restaurant Manager or General Manager may discreetly ask the Customer if the animal is a service animal, needed for a disability, but do not ask a customer to identify his or her disability;

D. In addition, do not ask for or demand proof of certification as a service animal;

2. Restaurant staff Employees should NOT require an individual with a disability to provide proof of a service animal's certification.

3. A notice shall be posted in all Shoney's, Inc. restaurants stating that individuals with disabilities are welcome, including those requiring the use of a service animal, i.e. seeing eye dog, hearing dog, etc.

4. Employees should direct any questions or clarification concerning this policy and procedure to the appropriate multi-unit management or the Field Human Resources department.

5. Businesses that sell or prepare food, such as Shoney's restaurants, must allow service animals in the public areas of their facilities, even if state or local health codes prohibit animals on the premises.

ENTRY OF JUDGMENT

Pending before the Court is Plaintiffs' Notice of Acceptance of Offer of Judgment from Defendant Shoney's LLC (Docket Entry No. 17). This Notice of Acceptance is accompanied by a certificate of service and a copy of the offer of judgment as made by Defendant Shoney's LLC and is submitted in compliance with the requirements of Fed. R. Civ. P. 68.

Accordingly, pursuant to Fed. R. Civ. P. 68, judgment is entered against Defendant Shoney's LLC in favor of Plaintiffs Nancy L. Gilliam and Charles Gilliam as follows:

1. $1000.00 (one-thousand dollars) with costs accrued as of the date of the Offer (July 13, 2006).

2. Attorneys fees in the amount of $5,518.16

3. Injunctive relief as specified in the Offer of Judgment in sections A, B & C.

Clerk of Court

APPENDIX 13:
ACCESSIBILITY GUIDELINES FOR NEW STADIUMS

ACCESSIBLE STADIUMS

The Americans with Disabilities Act (ADA) requires new stadiums to be accessible to people with disabilities so they, their families, and friends can enjoy equal access to entertainment, recreation, and leisure. This document highlights key accessibility requirements of the ADA that apply to new stadiums. Other accessibility requirements, such as those for parking lots, entrances, and rest rooms, also apply but these are the same as for other buildings. Compliance with all the accessibility requirements is essential to provide a basic level of access for people with disabilities.

To obtain a copy of the requirements for new stadiums and other facilities, contact the Department of Justice ADA Information Line at (800) 514-0301 voice or (800) 514-0383 TDD.

KEY FEATURES OF ACCESSIBLE STADIUMS

Seating

1. Wheelchair accessible seating is required. At least one percent of the seating must be wheelchair seating locations. Each wheelchair seating location is an open, level space that accommodates one person using a wheelchair and has a smooth, stable, and slip-resistant surface.

2. Accessible seating must be an integral part of the seating plan so that people using wheelchairs are not isolated from other spectators or their friends or family.

3. A companion seat must be provided next to each wheelchair seating location. The companion seat is a conventional seat that accommodates a friend or companion.

4. Wheelchair seating locations must be provided in all areas including sky boxes and specialty areas.

5. Removable or folding seats can be provided in wheelchair seating locations for use by persons who do not use wheelchairs so the facility does not lose revenue when not all wheelchair seating locations are ticketed to persons who use wheelchairs.

6. Whenever more than 300 seats are provided, wheelchair seating locations must be provided in more than one location. This is known as dispersed seating. Wheelchair seating locations must be dispersed throughout all seating areas and provide a choice of admission prices and views comparable to those for the general public.

7. Wheelchair seating locations must be on an accessible route that provides access from parking and transportation areas and that connects to all public areas, including concessions, restaurants, rest rooms, public telephones, and exits.

8. Wheelchair seating locations must provide lines of sight comparable to those provided to other spectators. In stadiums where spectators can be expected to stand during the show or event (for example, football, baseball, basketball games, or rock concerts), all or substantially all of the wheelchair seating locations must provide a line of sight over standing spectators. A comparable line of sight, as illustrated in the figure below, allows a person using a wheelchair to see the playing surface between the heads and over the shoulders of the persons standing in the row immediately in front and over the heads of the persons standing two rows in front.

9. In addition to wheelchair seating locations, at least one percent of all fixed seats in all seating areas must be aisle seats with no armrest, or with a removable or folding armrest, on the aisle side. These seats accommodate people who have a mobility disability but who wish to use a seat that is not a wheelchair seating location.

10. An accessible route must connect the wheelchair seating locations with the stage(s), performing areas, arena or stadium floor, dressing or locker rooms, and other spaces used by performers.

Concessions

All concessions, including food service areas, restaurants, and souvenir stands, must be accessible. For example, lowered counters must be provided where goods are provided and where cash registers are located. Condiments and self-serve food items must be provided within reach of a person using a wheelchair.

Access to playing fields, lockers, and spaces used by players and performers

An accessible route must provide access to all public and common use areas including the playing field, locker rooms, dugouts, stages, swimming pools, and warm-up areas. The accessible route provides access for the public, employees, and athletes using the facility.

Assistive Listening Systems

1. When audible communications are integral to the use of a stadium, assistive listening systems are required for people who are hard of hearing. These systems amplify sound and deliver it to a special receiver that is worn by the spectator, or connected to the spectator's hearing aid, depending on the type of system that is used.

2. The stadium must provide receivers for the assistive listening system. The number of available receivers must equal four percent of the total number of seats.

3. Signs must be provided to notify spectators of the availability of receivers for the assistive listening system.

OTHER ACCESSIBLE FEATURES

Accessible Parking Spaces

When parking spaces are provided, accessible parking spaces for cars and accessible parking spaces for vans are required. Accessible parking spaces must be the closest parking spaces to the accessible entrances and must be on an accessible route to the entrances.

Accessible Drop-Off and Pick-Up Areas

If passenger drop-off areas are provided, they must be accessible and an accessible route must connect each accessible drop-off area with the accessible entrance(s). Curb ramps must be provided if the drop-off area is next to a curb.

Accessible Entrances

1. At least fifty percent of the entrances must be accessible. Those that are not accessible must have signs that direct the public to the nearest accessible entrance.

2. Accessible entrances that have turnstiles must provide an accessible gate or door.

Rest Rooms

Each public and common use (including employee) rest room must be accessible. This includes rest rooms in work areas and rest rooms located in sky boxes and suites.

Public Telephones

1. Each bank of public telephones must have one or more wheelchair accessible telephones and these and other public telephones must have the ability to amplify the volume at the handset. A sign must identify telephones equipped with amplification.

2. At least one public TDD (telecommunications device for persons who are deaf or who have speech impairments) must be provided. Signs must identify the location of the TDD and provide direction from other telephone banks.

3. For each bank of public telephones with three or more units, at least one telephone must be equipped with a shelf and electrical outlet to permit a person to use a portable TDD.

Water Coolers or Drinking Fountains

Drinking fountains must accommodate people who use wheelchairs and people who stand but have difficulty bending or stooping. Half of the units must be wheelchair accessible and the others must accommodate standing users.

Visual Alarms

Where audible fire alarms or emergency notification is provided, flashing lights are required in public and common use areas, including toilet and bath rooms, locker rooms, and along public corridors.

Signs

Signs that identify permanent rooms and spaces, such as those identifying rest rooms, exits or room numbers, must have Braille and raised letters or numbers so that they may be read visually or tactually (by feeling the characters with one's fingers). They must also meet specific requirements for mounting location, color contrast, and non-glare surface. Signs that provide direction to, or information, about functional spaces must only comply with requirements for character proportion, character height, and finish and contrast between the characters and background.

APPENDIX 14:
DIRECTORY OF STATE SPEECH TO
SPEECH ACCESS SERVICES

STATE	ACCESS NUMBER
Alabama	1-800-229-5746
Alaska	1-866-355-6198
Arizona	1-800-842-6520
Arkansas	1-866-565-9823
California	1-800-854-7784
Colorado	1-877-659-4279
Connecticut	1-877-842-5177
Delaware	1-800-229-5746
District of Columbia	1-800-898-0740
Florida	1-877-955-5334
Georgia	1-888-202-4082
Hawaii	1-808-643-0787
Idaho	1-888-791-3004
Illinois	1-877-526-6690
Indiana	1-877-743-8231
Iowa	1-877-735-1007
Kansas	1-866-305-1344
Kentucky	1-888-244-6111

STATE	ACCESS NUMBER
Louisiana	1-888-272-5530
Maine	1-888-890-9256
Maryland	1-800-785-5630
Massachusetts	1-800-439-0183
Michigan	1-866-656-9826
Minnesota	1-877-627-3848
Mississippi	1-800-229-5746
Missouri	1-877-735-7877
Montana	1-877-253-4613
Nebraska	1-888-272-5527
Nevada	1-888-326-5658
New Hampshire	1-877-735-1245
New Jersey	1-800-229-5746
New Mexico	1-888-659-3952
New York	1-877-662-4234
North Carolina	1-877-735-8261
North Dakota	1-877-366-3709
Ohio	1-877-750-9097
Oklahoma	1-877-722-3515
Oregon	1-877-735-7525
Pennsylvania	1-800-229-5746
Rhode Island	1-866-355-9213
South Carolina	1-877-735-7277
South Dakota	1-877-981-9744
Tennessee	1-800-229-5746
Texas	1-877-826-6607
Utah	1-888-346-5822
Vermont	1-800-229-5746
Virginia	1-800-229-5746

Americans With Disabilities Act

STATE	ACCESS NUMBER
Washington	1-877-833-6341
West Virginia	1-800-229-5746
Wisconsin	1-800-833-7637
Wyoming	1-877-787-0503

SOURCE: Federal Communications Commission (FCC)

APPENDIX 15:
SETTLEMENT AGREEMENT BETWEEN THE UNITED STATES OF AMERICA AND GLENDALE, AZ POLICE DEPARTMENT - HEARING IMPAIRED SUSPECT

1. This matter was initiated by a complaint filed under title II of the Americans with Disabilities Act ("ADA"), 42 U.S.C. §§ 12131-12134, and section 504 of the Rehabilitation Act of 1973, as amended ("section 504") 29 U.S.C. § 794, with the United States Department of Justice ("Department of Justice")against the City of Glendale Police Department ("Police Department"). Allegedly, when the Glendale police officers arrested an individual who was deaf and used sign language for communication, he requested a sign language interpreter, but no interpreter was provided.

2. The Department of Justice is authorized under 28 C.F.R. Part 35, Subpart F, to investigate fully the allegations of the complaint in this matter to determine the Police Department's compliance of the Police Department with title II of the ADA and the Justice Department's implementing regulation, issue findings, and, where appropriate, negotiate and secure voluntary compliance agreements. Furthermore, the Attorney General is authorized under 42 U.S.C. § 12133, to bring a civil action enforcing title II of the ADA should the Department of Justice fail to secure voluntary compliance pursuant to Subpart F.

3. The parties to this Settlement Agreement are the United States of America and the Glendale Police Department. In consideration of the terms of this Agreement as set forth below, the Attorney General agrees to refrain from filing civil suit in this matter. In the interest of securing

compliance by voluntary means, the parties have entered into this Agreement and agree to the terms set forth below.

4. By signing this Agreement, the Police Department does not admit that the operation of its police services, policies, or practices violates in any respect the ADA or its implementing regulation.

5. The ADA applies to the Police Department because it is a public entity as defined in title II of the ADA and the title II regulation. 42 U.S.C. § 12115; and 28 C.F.R. § 35.104. Section 504 applies to the Police Department because it is a recipient as defined in section 504 and the Department of Justice's regulation implementing section 504. 29 U.S.C. § 794; and 28 C.F.R. § 42.540.

6. The subject of this Settlement Agreement is the provision of qualified interpreting services to ensure effective communication with individuals who are deaf or hard of hearing in various police situations.

7. The Police Department agrees to furnish appropriate auxiliary aids and services when necessary to afford an individual with a disability an equal opportunity to participate in, and enjoy the benefits of, the Police Department's services, programs, or activities. Auxiliary aids and services include qualified interpreters, written materials, and note pad and pen.

8. In any situation involving an individual who is deaf or hard of hearing, the Police Department agrees to give the individual the opportunity to request the auxiliary aid or service of his or her choice. The Police Department agrees to give primary consideration to the expressed choice of the individual unless the Police Department can demonstrate that another equally effective means of communication is available, or that use of the means chosen would result in a fundamental alteration in the service, program, or activity or in undue financial and administrative burdens.

9. Within 120 days of the effective date of this Agreement, the Police Department agrees that it will incorporate in its training program guidelines, which are attached, to provide that in those situations where the provision of interpreting services is necessary to ensure effective communication, the Police Department will secure such services.

10. Beginning on the effective date of this Agreement, the Police Department will instruct all of its employees who are in any way responsible for the provision of appropriate auxiliary aids and services, including qualified interpreters, to comply with the provisions of this Agreement.

11. Within 180 days of the effective date of this Agreement, the Police Department will conduct a training seminar for current personnel to

address the practical application of the ADA and this Agreement to police situations.

12. This Agreement is a public document. A copy of this document or any information contained in it, may be made available to any person. The Police Department will provide a copy of this Agreement to any person on request.

13. Failure by the Department of Justice to enforce this entire Agreement or any provision thereof with respect to any deadline or any other provision herein will not be construed as a waiver of its right to enforce other deadlines and provisions of this Agreement.

14. The effective date of this Agreement is the date of the last signature below.

15. This Agreement constitutes the entire agreement between the parties on the matters raised herein, and no other statement, promise, or agreement, either written or oral, made by either party or agents of either party, that is not contained in this written Agreement, will be enforceable under its provisions. This Agreement is limited to the facts set forth in the first paragraph, and it does not purport to remedy any other potential violations of the Americans with Disabilities Act or any other Federal law. This Agreement does not affect the Police Department's continuing responsibility to comply with all aspects of title II of the ADA.

For the Glendale Police
Department:

By: (Signature)
DAVID DOBROTKA
Chief of Police
Glendale, Arizona 85301

For the United States:

By: (Signature)
JOHN L. WODATCH, Chief
JOAN A. MAGAGNA, Deputy Chief
ROBERT J. MATHER, Attorney
Disability Rights Section
Civil Rights Division
U.S. Department of Justice
P.O. Box 66738
Washington, D.C. 20035-6738

GLENDALE POLICE DEPARTMENT
GUIDELINES FOR TRAINING ON
EFFECTIVE COMMUNICATION IN POLICE SITUATIONS
INVOLVING INDIVIDUALS WITH HEARING IMPAIRMENTS

Successful police contact with citizens is characterized by effective communication between the parties whether it is a suspect, victim, or complainant with whom the officer is talking. As such, police officers encountering an individual with hearing impairment should use appropriate auxiliary aids and services whenever necessary to ensure effective communication with the individual.

Auxiliary aids and services include qualified interpreters, written materials, note pads, and other effective methods of making aurally delivered materials available to individuals with hearing impairments.

When an auxiliary aid or service is required to ensure effective communication, the Glendale Police Department must provide an opportunity for individuals with hearing impairments to request the auxiliary aids and services of their choice and must give primary consideration to the choice expressed by the individuals. "Primary consideration" means that the Glendale Police Department must honor the choice, unless it can show that another equally effective means of communication is available, or that use of the means chosen would result in a fundamental alteration in the nature of its service, program, or activity or in undue financial and administrative burdens.

Police contact with citizens occurs most frequently during routine traffic stops. In situations involving drivers who are deaf and use sign language for communication, the officer should use appropriate sign language to initiate the exchange with the driver and should explain in writing the necessity for a stop and citation if the driver is to be charged with a traffic violation.

The officer may not ask a family member or friend of the driver to interpret.

These guidelines address only those situations where a police officer, after consulting with the individual with a hearing impairment, determines that the services of a qualified interpreter are necessary to ensure effective communication.

A. Arrest Upon Probable Cause Without An Interview

In circumstances where an individual without a hearing impairment would have been arrested on probable cause without an interview, then a suspect with a hearing impairment in the same situation usually does not need to be provided with a qualified interpreter. However, a qualified interpreter may be required if an officer is unable to convey to the arrestee the nature of the criminal charges by communicating on a note pad or by using another means of communication. The arrestee should be transported to a holding cell at the Public Safety Building where either the arresting officer or the transporting officer can convey the information through the interpreter when he or she arrives.

B. Interview Needed to Arrest Individual With A Hearing Impairment

If a police officer needs to interview a suspect with a hearing impairment to determine if there is probable cause to make an arrest, a qualified interpreter must be provided if the written communication is ineffective. When the services of a qualified interpreter are required to provide effective communication, but the officer cannot wait until a qualified interpreter arrives because the officer has to respond to another more urgent call, the following procedures apply:

1) If the investigation does not involve a serious offense, the officer must postpone the interview and possible arrest until the officer can return to the scene when a qualified interpreter is present. If this is not possible, the officer must document his or her investigation as completely as possible and file the appropriate report.

2) If the investigation involves a serious offense, the officer, before leaving the scene, must contact the appropriate Investigations Division supervisor and advise the supervisor of the case. The supervisor will determine if a detective will be called in to wait for a qualified interpreter. If not, the officer must document his or her investigation as completely as possible and file the appropriate report.

C. Interrogating An Arrestee With A Hearing Impairment

If an officer cannot effectively inform the arrestee of the Miranda warnings without the use of an interpreter, then the officer must secure the services of a qualified interpreter in order to communicate accurately the warnings to the arrestee prior to any interrogation. An officer seeking to interrogate an arrestee with a hearing impairment must obtain the services of a qualified interpreter prior to any interrogation whenever an interpreter is needed for effective communication. If exigent circumstances do not permit a delay in the interrogation of the arrestee, if an interpreter cannot be located within a reasonable period of time (which should occur very infrequently), if written communication between the officer and the arrestee was effective in conveying an understanding of the Miranda warnings, or if the arrestee specifically declines the opportunity to communicate through an interpreter, the officer may proceed with the interrogation by using a note pad. However, if written communication becomes ineffective, for example, because the factual pattern is complex, because the arrestee is having difficulty communicating without an interpreter, or because the arrestee chooses to discontinue the interrogation, the officer must discontinue the interrogation and wait until a qualified interpreter is present before continuing the interrogation. In most instances a qualified interpreter will be available and the interrogation will not be delayed.

D. Issuance of Appearance Ticket

In circumstances in which an individual without a hearing impairment would be issued an appearance ticket without being questioned by the investigating officer, then a suspect with a hearing impairment in the same situation does not need to be provided with a qualified interpreter. If an officer has stopped a suspect for committing a non-criminal infraction and if the officer is unable to convey to the violator the nature of the non-criminal infraction by communicating on a note pad or by using another means of communication, then the officer should use his or her discretion as to whether to call a qualified interpreter to the scene or whether to issue a warning rather than a citation.

E. Interviewing A Victim or Critical Witness With A Hearing Impairment

If an officer is able to communicate effectively by writing questions on a note pad and having the victim or witness with a hearing impairment write his or her responses, then the officer may proceed with the interview using a note pad. However, if an investigating officer is unable to communicate effectively with a victim or critical witness by using a note pad or some other means of communication other than a qualified interpreter, then the investigating officer must provide the victim or critical witness with a qualified interpreter. If the investigating officer cannot wait until a qualified interpreter arrives because the officer has to respond to another more urgent call, the following procedures apply:

1) If the investigation does not involve a serious offense, then (a) the officer can have a qualified interpreter dispatched to the victim's or critical witness's location and request the dispatcher re-contact the officer when the interpreter arrives. If a qualified interpreter is unable

to respond or if the officer cannot return to the scene, the officer must document his or her investigation as completely as possible and file the appropriate report; or (b) the officer can ask the victim or critical witness to come voluntarily to the section office when a qualified interpreter is available. At that time, the investigating officer can return to the station to complete the investigation. If a qualified interpreter is unable to respond or if the officer cannot return to the station, the officer must document his or her investigation as completely as possible and file the appropriate report.

2) If the investigation does involve a serious offense and if the victim or witness with a hearing impairment is critical to establishing probable cause for an arrest or for completing the investigation, then the investigating officer, before leaving the scene, must contact his or her supervisor and advise the supervisor of the case. The supervisor will determine if an investigator will be called in to wait for a qualified interpreter. If the supervisor determines that an investigator will not be responding; and if neither option (1)(a) nor (1)(b) above is available, then the officer may leave the victim(s) or witness(es) at the scene. The investigating officer must then document his or her investigation as completing as possible and file the report.

F. Obtaining Qualified Interpreters

Officers will arrange for a qualified interpreter the Valley Center for the deaf and request that a qualified interpreter be provided. If the person requests an interpreter other than from the Valley Center for the Deaf, the request should be honored if the interpreter is available and qualified.

G. Reports/Evidence

All identifying information on the interpreter must be included in the report, including the interpreter's name, the time the interpreter was called, and his/her time of arrival and departure. All written questions and responses between and among police officers and persons with hearing impairments must be treated as evidence and handled accordingly.

GLOSSARY

Accommodation—A term used in the context of public accommodations and facilities that an individual with a disability may not be excluded, denied services, segregated or otherwise treated differently than other individuals by a public accommodation or commercial facility.

Achievement levels—Achievement levels define what students should know and be able to do at different levels of performance as follows: (1) Basic level denotes partial mastery of prerequisite knowledge and skills that are fundamental for proficient work at each grade; (2) Proficient level represents solid academic performance for each grade assessed, and competency over challenging subject matter, including subject-matter knowledge, application of such knowledge to real-world situations, and analytical skills appropriate to the subject matter; (3) Advanced level signifies superior performance.

Action at Law—A judicial proceeding whereby one party prosecutes another for a wrong done.

Actual Damages—Actual damages are those damages directly referable to the breach or tortious act, and which can be readily proven to have been sustained, and for which the injured party should be compensated as a matter of right.

Air Carrier Access Act—Statute prohibiting discrimination by air carriers against qualified individuals with physical or mental impairments.

Alternative Keyboard—Alternative keyboards may be different from standard keyboards in size, shape, layout, or function. They offer individuals with special needs greater efficiency, control, and comfort.

Alternative Schools—Alternative schools serve students whose needs cannot be met in a regular, special education, or vocational school, e.g., schools for potential dropouts; residential treatment centers for substance abuse; schools for chronic truants; and schools for students with behavioral problems.

Ambulation Aids—Devices that help people walk upright, including canes, crutches, and walkers.

American Civil Liberties Union (ACLU)—A nationwide organization dedicated to the enforcement and preservation of rights and civil liberties guaranteed by the federal and state constitutions.

Americans with Disabilities Act (ADA)—A federal law which prohibits discrimination on the basis of a "qualified" disability as set forth in the statute.

Americans with Disability Act Accessibility Guidelines (ADAAG)—Technical standard for accessible design of new construction or alterations adopted by the Department of Justice for places of public accommodation pursuant to Title III of the ADA.

A Nation at Risk—A report published by the U.S. Department of Education in highlighting deficiencies in knowledge of the nation's students and population as a whole in areas such as literacy, mathematics, geography, and basic science.

Appropriations—Budget authority provided through the congressional appropriation process that permits federal agencies to incur obligations and to make payments.

Architectural Barrier—A physical feature of a public accommodation that limits or prevents disabled persons from obtaining the goods or services offered.

Architectural Barriers Act (ABA)—A federal law requiring that buildings and facilities that are designed, constructed or altered with federal funds, or leased by a federal agency, must comply with Federal standards for physical accessibility by the disabled.

Assistive Technology Device—Any item, piece of equipment, or product system, whether acquired commercially off the shelf, modified, or customized, that is used to increase, maintain, or improve functional capabilities of a child with a disability.

Assistive Technology Service—Any service that directly assists a child with a disability in the selection, acquisition, or use of an assistive technology device.

At-risk—Being "at-risk" means having one or more family background or other risk factors that have been found to predict a high rate of school failure—e.g., retention or dropping out—at some time in the future, including having a mother whose education is less than high school, living in a single-parent family, receiving welfare assistance, and living in a household where the primary language spoken is other than English.

Augmentative Communication System—Any system that increases or improves communication of individuals with receptive or expressive communication impairments. The system can include speech, gestures, sign language, symbols, synthesized speech, dedicated communication devices, microcomputers, and other communication systems.

Back Pay—Wages awarded to an employee who was illegally discharged.

Braille—A raised dot printed language that is used by persons with visual impairments. Each raised dot configuration represents a letter or word combination.

Braille Embossers and Translators—A Braille embosser transfers computer-generated text into embossed braille output. Translation programs convert text scanned in or generated via standard word processing programs into Braille that can be printed on the embosser.

Burden of Proof—The duty of a party to substantiate an allegation or issue to convince the trier of fact as to the truth of their claim.

Bureau of Labor Statistics—A division of the U.S. Department of Labor that compiles statistics related to employment.

Capacity—Capacity is the legal qualification concerning the ability of one to understand the nature and effects of one's acts.

Captioning—A text transcript of the audio portion of multimedia products, such as video and television, that is synchronized to the visual events taking place on screen.

Child Abuse—Any form of cruelty to a child's physical, moral or mental well-being.

Child Protective Agency—A state agency responsible for the investigation of child abuse and neglect reports.

Child Welfare—A generic term that embraces the totality of measures necessary for a child's well being; physical, moral and mental.

Child Aged 3 Through 9—The term "child with a disability" for a child aged 3 through 9 may, at the discretion of the State and the local educational agency, include a child: (i) experiencing developmental delays, as defined by the State and as measured by appropriate diagnostic instruments and procedures, in one or more of the following areas: physical development, cognitive development, communication development, social or emotional development, or adaptive development; and (ii) who, by reason thereof, needs special education and related services.

Child With a Disability—In general, refers to a child: (i) with mental retardation, hearing impairments including deafness, speech or language impairments, visual impairments including blindness, serious emotional disturbance, orthopedic impairments, autism, traumatic brain injury, other health impairments, or specific learning disabilities; and (ii) who, by reason thereof, needs special education and related services.

Circumstantial Evidence—Indirect evidence by which a principal fact may be inferred.

Civil Rights of Institutionalized Persons Act (CRIPA)—Statute intended to monitor the health and safety of individuals confined in State and local government correctional facilities, nursing homes and mental institutions.

Community Development Block Grant Program (CDBGP)—A federal program administered by the U.S. Department of Housing and Urban Development (HUD), which provides funding to public entities for the purpose of taking measures to facilitate access for the disabled population to the entity's services and programs.

Compensatory Revenue—A type of categorical revenue that targets resources to school districts for instruction and other supplemental services for educationally disadvantaged students.

Constitution—The fundamental principles of law that frame a governmental system.

Constitutional Right—Refers to the individual liberties granted by the constitution of a state or the federal government.

Corporal Punishment—Physical punishment as distinguished from pecuniary punishment or a fine; any kind of punishment of, or inflicted on, the body.

Court—The branch of government responsible for the resolution of disputes arising under the laws of the government.

Damages—In general, damages refers to monetary compensation which the law awards to one who has been injured by the actions of another, such as in the case of tortious conduct or breach of contractual obligations.

Delinquent—An infant of not more than a specified age who has violated criminal laws or has engaged in disobedient, indecent or immoral conduct, and is in need of treatment, rehabilitation, or supervision.

Disability—Under the ADA, an individual is considered disabled if he or she (i) is substantially impaired with respect to a major life activity; (ii) has a record of such an impairment; or (iii) is regarded as having an impairment.

Digitized Speech—Human speech that is recorded onto an integrated circuit chip and which has the ability to be played back.

Display—Assistive technology that raises or lowers dot patterns based on input from an electronic device such as a screen reader or text browser.

Due Process Rights—All rights that are of such fundamental importance as to require compliance with due process standards of fairness and justice.

Duty—The obligation, to which the law will give recognition and effect, to conform to a particular standard of conduct toward another.

Educational Attainment—The highest level of schooling attended and completed.

Educational Service Agency—Refers to (A) a regional public multi-service agency: (i) authorized by State law to develop, manage, and provide services or programs to local educational agencies; and (ii) recognized as an administrative agency for purposes of the provision of special education and related services provided within public elementary and secondary schools of the State; and (B) includes any other public institution or agency having administrative control and direction over a public elementary or secondary school.

Electronic Pointing Devices—Electronic pointing devices allow the user to control the cursor on the screen using ultrasound, an infrared beam, eye movements, nerve signals, or brains waves. When used with an on-screen keyboard, electronic pointing devices also allow the user to enter text or data.

Elementary School—A nonprofit institutional day or residential school that provides elementary education, as determined under state law.

English as a Second Language (ESL)—Programs that provide intensive instruction in English for students with limited English proficiency.

Enrollment—The total number of students registered in a given school unit at a given time, generally in the fall of a year.

Environmental Control Unit (ECU)—A system that enables individuals to control various electronic devices in their environment through a variety of alternative access methods, such as switch or voice access. Target devices include lights, televisions, telephones, music players, door openers, security systems, and kitchen appliances. Also referred to as Electronic Aid to Daily Living (EADL).

Equal access—Equal opportunity of a qualified person with a disability to participate in or benefit from educational aids, benefits, or services.

Equipment—The term "equipment" includes (A) machinery, utilities, and built-in equipment and any necessary enclosures or structures to house such machinery, utilities, or equipment; and (B) all other items necessary for the functioning of a particular facility as a facility for the provision of educational services, including items such as instructional equipment and necessary furniture; printed, published, and audio-visual instructional materials; telecommunications, sensory, and other technological aids and devices; and books, periodicals, documents, and other related materials.

Excess Costs—Those costs that are in excess of the average annual per-student expenditure in a local educational agency during the preceding school year for an elementary or secondary school student, as may be appropriate, and which shall be computed after deducting (A) amounts received: (i) under part B of this title; (ii) under part A of title I of the Elementary and Secondary Education Act of 1965; or (iii) under part A of title VII of that Act; and (B) any State or local funds expended for programs that would qualify for assistance under any of those parts.

Fair Housing Act—Statute prohibiting housing discrimination on the basis of race, color, religion, sex, national origin, familial status, and disability.

Free Appropriate Public Education—A term used in the elementary and secondary school context; refers to the provision of regular or special education and related aids and services that are designed to meet individual educational needs of students with disabilities as adequately as the needs of students without disabilities are met and is based upon adherence to procedures that satisfy the Section 504 requirements pertaining to educational setting, evaluation and placement, and procedural safeguards.

Guardian—A person who is entrusted with the management of the property and/or person of another who is incapable, due to age or incapacity, to administer their own affairs.

Hearing Impairment—An impairment in hearing, whether permanent or fluctuating, that adversely affects a child's educational performance, in the most severe case, because the child is impaired in processing linguistic information through hearing.

High school—A secondary school offering the final years of high school work necessary for graduation.

Indian—An individual who is a member of an Indian tribe.

Indian Tribe—Any Federal or State Indian tribe, band, rancheria, pueblo, colony, or community, including any Alaskan Native village or regional village corporation (as defined in or established under the Alaska Native Claims Settlement Act).

Individualized Education Program (IEP)—A written statement for each child with a disability that is developed, reviewed, and revised in accordance with section 1414(d).

Individuals with Disabilities Education Act (IDEA)—A statute requiring public schools to provide a free public education to disabled children in the least restrictive environment appropriate for the child's needs.

In Loco Parentis—Latin for "in the place of a parent." Refers to an individual who assumes parental obligations and status without a formal, legal adoption.

Infancy—The period prior to reaching the legal age of majority.

Judge—The individual who presides over a court, and whose function it is to determine controversies.

Keyguards—Keyguards are hard plastic covers with holes for each key. Using a keyguard, someone with an unsteady finger or with a pointing device can avoid striking unwanted keys.

Local Educational Agency—A public board of education or other public authority legally constituted within a State for either administrative control or direction of, or to perform a service function for, public elementary or secondary schools in a city, county, township, school district, or other political subdivision of a State, or for such combination of school districts or counties as are recognized in a State as an administrative agency for its public elementary or secondary schools.

Minor—A person who has not yet reached the age of majority.

Modal Grade—The modal grade is the year of school in which the largest proportion of students of a given age are enrolled and classified according to their relative progress in school, i.e., whether the grade or year in which they were enrolled was below, at, or above the modal or typical grade for persons of their age at the time of the survey.

Multiple disabilities—Concomitant impairments—e.g., mental retardation- blindness, mental retardation-orthopedic impairment, etc.—the combination of which causes such severe educational problems that they cannot be accommodated in special education programs solely for one of the impairments. The term does not include deaf-blindness.

Native Language—With reference to an individual of limited English proficiency, means the language normally used by the individual, or in the case of a child, the language normally used by the parents of the child.

Nonprofit—With reference to a school, agency, organization, or institution, means a school, agency, organization, or institution owned and operated by one or more nonprofit corporations or associations no part of the net earnings of which inures, or may lawfully inure, to the benefit of any private shareholder or individual.

Occupational Education—Refers to vocational education programs that prepare students for a specific occupation or cluster of occupations, including agriculture, business, marketing, health care, protective services, trade and industrial, technology, food service, child care, and personal and other services programs.

Onscreen Keyboard—On-screen keyboards are software images of a standard or modified keyboard placed on the computer screen by software. The keys are selected by a mouse, touch screen, trackball, joystick, switch, or electronic pointing device.

Optical Character Recognition and Scanners—Optical character recognition (OCR) software works with a scanner to convert images from a printed page into a standard computer file. A scanner is a device that converts an image from a printed page to a computer file. With optical character recognition software, the resulting computer file can be edited.

Orthopedic Impairments—Refers to a severe orthopedic impairment that adversely affects a child's educational performance, including impairments caused by congenital anomaly, e.g., clubfoot, absence of some member, etc.; impairments caused by disease, e.g., poliomyelitis, bone tuberculosis, etc.; and impairments from other causes, e.g., cerebral palsy, amputations, and fractures or burns that cause contractures.

Other Support Services Staff—Refers to all staff not reported in other categories, including media personnel, social workers, data processors, health maintenance workers, bus drivers, security, cafeteria workers, and other staff.

Outlying Areas—Includes the United States Virgin Islands, Guam, American Samoa, and the Commonwealth of the Northern Mariana Islands.

Parens Patriae—Latin for "parent of his country." Refers to the role of the state as guardian of legally disabled individuals.

Parent—The term "parent" (A) includes a legal guardian; and (B) except as used in sections 1415(b)(2) and 1439(a)(5), includes an individual assigned under either of those sections to be a surrogate parent.

Placement—A term used in the elementary and secondary school context; refers to a regular and/or special educational program in which a student receives educational and/or related services.

Prima Facie Case—A case which is sufficient on its face, being supported by at least the requisite minimum of evidence, and being free from palpable defects.

Public Entities—For the purposes of Title II coverage under the ADA, refers to state and local governments, their departments, agencies or other instrumentalities.

Reading literacy—Reading literacy is defined as understanding, using, and reflecting on written texts in order to achieve one's goals, to develop one's knowledge and potential, and to participate in society.

Reasonable accommodation—A term used in the employment context to refer to modifications or adjustments employers make to a job application process, the work environment, the manner or circumstances under which the position held or desired is customarily performed, or that enable a covered entity's employee with a disability to enjoy equal benefits and privileges of employment.

Regular School Districts—A regular school district can be either: (1) a school district that is not a component of a supervisory union; or (2) a school district component of a supervisory union that shares a superintendent and administrative services with other local school districts.

Regular schools—Schools that are part of state and local school systems as well as private elementary/secondary schools, both religiously affiliated and nonsectarian, that are not alternative schools, vocational education schools, special education schools, subcollegiate departments of postsecondary institutions, residential schools for exceptional children, federal schools for American Indians or Alaska Natives, or federal schools on military posts and other federal installations.

Rehabilitation Act of 1973—A disability discrimination statute that preceded and served as a model for the ADA.

Reinstatement—Refers to the return of an employee to employment from which he or she was illegally dismissed.

Related Services—Refers to transportation, and such developmental, corrective, and other supportive services, including speech-language pathology and audiology services, psychological services, physical and occupational therapy, recreation, including therapeutic recreation, social work services, counseling services, including rehabilitation counseling, orientation and mobility services, and medical services, except that such medical services shall be for diagnostic and evaluation purposes only as may be required to assist a child with a disability to benefit from special education, and includes the early identification and assessment of disabling conditions in children.

Remedial Education—Instruction for a student lacking the reading, writing, mathematics, or other skills necessary to perform college-level work at the level required by the attended institution.

Scale score—Uses a set scale to assess overall achievement in a domain, such as mathematics.

School District—Also referred to as a local education agency (LEA), refers to an education agency at the local level that exists primarily to operate public schools or to contract for public school services.

Screen Enlargement Programs—Screen enlargement programs magnify a portion of the screen, increasing the visibility for some users with limited vision. Most have variable magnification levels. Some screen enlargement programs offer text-to-speech.

Screen Reader—A screen reader is a software program that uses synthesized speech to "speak" graphics and text out loud. This type of program is used by people with limited vision or blindness.

Seating and Positioning Aids—Modifications to wheelchairs or other seating systems that provide greater body stability, upright posture or reduction of pressure on the skin surface.

Secondary School—A nonprofit institutional day or residential school that provides secondary education, as determined under State law, except that it does not include any education beyond grade 12.

Secretary—The term ` "Secretary" as used herein refers to the Secretary of Education.

Service Animal—Refers to an animal, such as a guide dog, which has been trained to provide assistance to disabled individuals.

Special education schools—Special education schools provide educational services to students with special physical or mental needs—i.e., students with mental disabilities (such as mental retardation or autism); physical disabilities (such as hearing impairments); or learning disabilities (such as dyslexia).

Specific learning disabilities: A disorder in one or more of the basic psychological processes involved in understanding or in using language, spoken or written, that may manifest itself in an imperfect ability to listen, think, speak, read, write, spell, or do mathematical calculations, including such conditions as perceptual disabilities, brain injury, minimal brain dysfunction, dyslexia, and developmental aphasia. The term does not apply to children who have learning problems that are primarily the result of visual, hearing, or motor disabilities; of mental retardation; of emotional disturbance; or of environmental, cultural, or economic disadvantage.

Speech or language impairments—A communication disorder such as stuttering, impaired articulation, a language impairment, or a voice impairment that adversely affects a child's educational performance.

Standing—The legal right of an individual or group to use the courts to resolve an existing controversy.

State—Refers to each of the 50 States, the District of Columbia, the Commonwealth of Puerto Rico, and each of the outlying areas.

State Educational Agency—The State board of education or other agency or officer primarily responsible for the State supervision of public elementary and secondary schools, or, if there is no such officer or agency, an officer or agency designated by the Governor or by State law.

Status Offender—A child who commits an act which is not criminal in nature, but which nevertheless requires some sort of intervention and disciplinary attention merely because of the age of the offender.

Statute of Limitations—Any law that fixes the time within which parties must take judicial action to enforce rights or thereafter be barred from enforcing them.

Supplementary Aids and Services—Refers to aids, services, and other supports that are provided in regular education classes or other education-related settings to enable children with disabilities to be educated with nondisabled children to the maximum extent appropriate under the applicable statute.

Supreme Court—In most jurisdictions, the Supreme Court is the highest appellate court, including the federal court system.

Talking Word Processors—A talking word processor is a software program that uses synthesized speech to provide auditory feedback of what has been typed.

Tax Credits and Deductions -Incentives offered to businesses to encourage compliance with the ADA by providing tax credits or deductions to offset the cost of undertaking initiatives to make their establishments and services accessible to the disabled population

Telecommunications Device for the Deaf (TDD)—An auxiliary aid consisting of a keyboard and display which is attached to a telephone and used by individuals with hearing or speech impairments to communicate on the telephone.

Telecommunications Relay Services (TRS)—A service that enables hearing or speech-impaired callers to communicate with each other through a third party communications assistant using a TDD.

Telephone Emergency Services -Basic emergency services, such as police, fire and ambulance services, that are provided by public safety agencies, including the "911" system.

Termination—Refers to cessation of employment, e.g. by quitting or dismissal.

Traditional Public School—All public schools that are not public charter schools or Bureau of Indian Affairs-funded schools operated by local public school districts, including regular, special education, vocational/technical, and alternative schools.

Transition Services—Refers to a coordinated set of activities for a student with a disability that (A) are designed within an outcome-oriented process, which promotes movement from school to post-school activities, including post-secondary education, vocational training, integrated employment, including supported employment, continuing and adult education, adult services, independent living, or community participation; (B) are based upon the individual student's needs, taking into account the student's preferences and interests; and (C) include instruction, related services, community experiences, the development of employment and other post-school adult living objectives, and, when appropriate, acquisition of daily living skills and functional vocational evaluation.

Truancy—Willful and unjustified failure to attend school by one who is required to attend.

TTD or TTY—A Telecommunication Device for the Deaf (TTY or TDD) is a device with a keyboard that sends and receives typed messages over a telephone line.

Unconstitutional—Refers to a statute which conflicts with the United States Constitution rendering it void.

Uniform Federal Accessibility Standard (UFAS)—Technical standard for accessible design of new construction and alterations pursuant to the Architectural Barriers Act.

U.S. Equal Employment Opportunity Commission (EEOC)—Federal agency responsible for issuing regulations to enforce the provisions of Title I of the ADA.

Vocational Education Schools—Vocational schools primarily serve students who are being trained for semi-skilled or technical occupations.

Voice Recognition—Voice recognition allows the user to speak to the computer instead of using a keyboard or mouse to input data or control computer functions.

Wrongful Discharge—An unlawful dismissal of an employee.

BIBLIOGRAPHY AND ADDITIONAL RESOURCES

American Civil Liberties Union (ACLU) Department of Public Education (Date Visited: September 2007) http://www.aclu.org/

Black's Law Dictionary, Fifth Edition. St. Paul, MN: West Publishing Company, 1979.

The Office of Fair Housing and Equal Opportunity (Date Visited: September 2007) http://www.fairhousingfirst.org

The U.S. Census Bureau (Date Visited: September 2007) http://www.census.gov/

The U.S. Department of Education (Date Visited: September 2007) http://www.ed.gov/

The U.S. Department of Housing and Urban Development (Date Visited: September 2007) http://www.hud.gov/

The U.S. Department of Justice (Date Visited: September 2007) http://www.usdoj.gov/

The U.S. Department of Labor (Date Visited: September 2007) http://www.dol.gov/

The U.S. Department of Transportation (Date Visited: September 2007) http://www.dot.gov/

The U.S. Equal Opportunity Commission (Date Visited: September 2007) http://www.eeoc.gov/

The U.S. General Resources Administration, Center for IT Accommodation (CITA) (Date Visited: September 2007) http://www.gsa.gov/section508

The U.S. Social Security Administration (Date Visited: September 2007) http://www.ssa.gov/